The Albert Plan To Restore Election Integrity

DAN ALBERT

Published by: Freedom Cell Publishing, Inc., Greenville, SC

ISBN: 978-1-953014-02-3

Cover design by: Jan Shade Beach
All Bible references are from the King James Version
TheAlbertPlan@gmail.com
FreedomCells.com

To the heroes who will inspire millions to engage in the fight to restore election integrity to our great nation. May God guide us and strengthen us in our effort to save our Republic and to preserve the light of liberty for our posterity and all mankind.

CONTENTS

Introduction.. 1

The 2020 Election Farce.. 5

Restore Integrity to Federal Elections 23

Show Me the Evidence! 41

Clear and Present Danger... 65

A Call to Action 81

The Clamoring 103

The Clamoring: Part 2.. 127

Next Steps.. 149

Election Integrity Survey 157

2020 Freedom Cell Survey 161

Introduction

Watching events unfold leading up to the November 3, 2020 election, and for several months afterward, was like watching a slow motion train wreck. You could see it coming, but there was nothing that you could do about it but watch. Every honest person with the slightest amount of intellectual curiosity could see that the 2020 election was a farce.

Millions of unsolicited absentee ballots were mailed to voters on dirty voter rolls. What could possibly go wrong with that? State election laws were being changed or ignored, and ballot boxes were being deployed to collect absentee ballots, sometimes from people that were able to vote without presenting proper identification.

The perpetrators of the fraud were quite open about it. From his basement, Joe Biden said "We have put together, I think, the most extensive and inclusive voter fraud organization in the history of American politics." Hillary Clinton told him not to concede under any circumstances, and the "nonpartisan" Transition Integrity Project gamed out how they would assure that Joe Biden would be declared the winner. We were told that the "red mirage" of a Trump win on election night would be erased in the hours and days that followed.

Election laws were violated with impunity. Republican observers were denied the opportunity for meaningful observation of the election process. Fox News called the Arizona election for Joe Biden when there was no basis to call it so early on election night with so many votes left to count. States that were too close to call stopped counting votes almost simultaneously in the middle of the night, followed by implausibly large ballot dumps that were heavily skewed in favor of Joe Biden, a man that campaigned from his basement because he was too feeble to get out on the campaign trail. The fix was in!

Integrity in elections is very simple to design and implement, if there is a desire to do so. We the People must pursue an "all of the above" strategy to eliminate every opportunity for nefarious actors to commit election fraud or voter fraud.

By decoupling federal elections from state and local elections, we can simplify the election process so that a separate paper ballot can be used for each decision made in a federal election. Paper ballots can be sorted by race and counted quickly and accurately at each precinct after polls close on election night.

Federal Election Day can be held in November of even-numbered years and state and local elections can be held during odd-numbered years. We can solve chain of custody issues with ballots by eliminating early voting and absentee voting, and we can have full transparency by live streaming the election process at each precinct. We can use fingerprints to eliminate the possibility of ballots being discarded or inserted into the ballot box, while still preserving the secret vote.

Restoring election integrity is the seminal issue of our time, for without election integrity, our nation becomes a banana republic, and we are no longer governed by the consent of the governed. We the People must organize ourselves to move as one and speak as one. The silent majority must become the clamoring majority.

In *The Albert Plan to Save America: 2020 Edition*, I laid out the bold, comprehensive, transformational plan that We the People must implement to restore election integrity, to restore federalism, to restore national sovereignty, to restore individual liberty, to restore limited government, and to unleash free-market capitalism. The solutions are simple, they just aren't easy. Everything in *The Albert Plan* depends upon first restoring election integrity.

Liberty is decentralized and distributed, so by taking a cellular approach and forming self-organizing, autonomous Freedom Cells in any configuration that we might find useful, 30 million patriots can organize for action in order to save our Republic. By organizing Freedom Cells in sufficient numbers at every election precinct, We the People can overwhelm and transform the Republican Party. We need not form a third party to repudiate the entrenched establishment political class; we simply need to form Freedom Cells to function as the Freedom Caucus of the Republican Party.

By becoming "the clamoring majority," We the People must clamor for the implementation of this very simple plan to restore election integrity while also clamoring for getting to the bottom of what happened during the 2020 Election Farce. We must clamor for state legislators to grow a backbone and conduct full forensic audits of the 2020 election to the extent that it is possible to do so, and for our states to exercise our tenth amendment rights to push back against a tyrannical federal government.

We the People must not stop at restoring election integrity, we must also clamor for all of the elements of *The Albert Plan* in order to restore American exceptionalism. We must not allow the American experiment to come to an end, and for the light of liberty to be extinguished. Our nation is in great distress, but there is also a great opportunity for national renewal and revival.

ONE

The 2020 Election Farce

THE UNITED STATES HAS BECOME A BANANA REPUBLIC

We have put together, I think, the most extensive and inclusive voter fraud organization in the history of American politics.

— Joe Biden

Millions of patriots could see it coming, but nobody that had any authority to do anything about it had the will and the opportunity to stop it. The stage was set for the greatest election fraud in history because Democrats were allowed for decades to get away with incremental encroachments upon election integrity.

A FALSE NARRATIVE

Democrats and others that want to undermine election integrity seem to have no problem getting on the same page and constantly repeating the false narratives that they have used successfully in the past to force incremental changes to our election system that chip away at election integrity. Lockstep liars can be subtle in their deceitfulness at times, and at other times they are very bold. At times it is a small twist of the truth. Sometimes it is a lie so outlandish that it gains acceptance after constant repetition.

Count Every Vote

The Democrat mantra to "count every vote" may sound good on the surface, but what they really mean by that phrase is to count every vote regardless of whether or not the vote was legally cast by a United States citizen eligible to vote. As the party of deception, the Democrat party repeats lies such as this one until the phrase is embedded in the minds of uninformed people that blindly accept it as a statement of truth.

Those that seek the truth and speak the truth quickly recognize this lie and counter with "count every legal vote," which should be readily accepted by all patriotic Americans, but Democrats spew the lie that anyone using such a phrase is a white supremacist that is seeking to suppress the votes of the oppressed victim groups on the Democrat plantation.

Democrats use this mantra in hopes that the average person will blindly accept their assertion that counting should continue of all votes that they managed to stuff into ballot boxes regardless of how egregious their methods of fraud are.

Lies like these are part and parcel to the Democrat effort to undermine election integrity and to enforce party discipline to get lockstep liars on the same page. They think that all Americans are stupid or cower when threatened with absurd accusations of white supremacy, systemic racism and other tired phrases that are losing their punch.

Everyone Should Vote

During an interview with one of his guests on his show, Wolf Blitzer stated that "everyone should vote." This is another Democrat party mantra that is repeated ad nauseam in order to try to ingrain in the minds of uninformed voters that it would be a good thing if everyone voted, that everyone should vote, and that any measure used to maximize the percentage of voters that vote would be a good thing.

What Democrats fail to mention is that they use this phrase not only to justify measures that would maximize voter turnout at the expense of election integrity, but they provide cover for themselves for when they miraculously turn out 100% or more of voters in numerous Democrat-controlled election jurisdictions.

It is reported that even in countries where voting is mandatory, election turnout seldom exceeds 80% to 90% of eligible voters. There are many reasons for people not to vote, and it is personal choice whether they vote or not. Some people don't care who wins elected office in the races that they could vote for. Some people abstain from voting because they don't believe in the process at all, such as agorists. Some people refrain from voting altogether or for a particular office because they know that they are uninformed about the candidates and the issues. Some people don't value their vote enough to inconvenience themselves to show up to vote at their polling location.

Democrats say they want everyone to vote, and that everyone should vote, but they are only interested in maximizing the number of votes for their candidates. They thrive on the uninformed voter voting for Democrat candidates. They thrive on the votes of people that are dependent upon government assistance.

Voting Should be Easy

In the same interview, Wolf Blitzer made the statement that voting should be as easy as possible. This is another Democrat mantra that they would like to pursue with no regard for the impact on election integrity. At a time when it is obvious that we need to move away from electronic voting and electronic tabulation of votes, Democrats would have us move toward online voting by anyone, at any time, coupled with the electronic tabulation of votes that could be easily manipulated by a handful of people.

In their quest to obliterate election integrity altogether, Democrats are insidious in their incremental approach to chipping away at any means by which We the People could be assured of fair, free, honest, and transparent elections. Democrats made a great leap forward in their effort to make voting easier in the 2020 election by mailing out unsolicited ballots, expanding absentee and early voting, and the implementation of ballot drop boxes.

Playing the Race Card

Democrats routinely play the race card in order to guilt or shame Republican voters and candidates. The fact of the matter is that that tactic is worn out, and We the People have recognized the truth that anyone that plays the race card is indeed a racist. The only systemic racism in this country that I have observed in decades is within the Democrat party. Democrats have overused this tactic in pursuing election fraud.

Voter Suppression

Like the boy that cried wolf too many times, Democrats have overused accusations of "voter suppression." They almost always couple this accusation with playing the race card, which is in and of itself a racist act, for making the accusation they imply that members of their victim groups are stupid or incompetent. If we want voter ID because it makes the election more secure, they scream "voter suppression." They assert that somehow the votes of our black brothers and sisters are suppressed because they either don't have IDs or can't easily get IDs.

Any measure that we might propose to improve election integrity will elicit charges like voter suppression from Democrats. The only votes that truth-seeking and truth-speaking patriots would like to suppress are illegal votes. Every honest American should desire the same thing.

Limited Cases of Election Fraud

Another lie repeated by Democrats is that there are limited cases of election fraud or voter fraud. Election fraud and voter fraud were rampant even before the 2020 election, yet the 2020 election took election fraud to a staggering level. If Democrats truly believed that there was limited election fraud or voter fraud, they would not object to taking every reasonable measure to improve and assure election integrity.

Numerous cases of election fraud and voter fraud are prosecuted, but the truth is that they amount to a very small percentage of what is actually perpetrated by nefarious actors. If Democrats had their way, we wouldn't see prosecutions of voter fraud and election fraud at all.

If a Democrat administration stops apprehending people that cross the border illegally, would such a small number of apprehensions mean that there were very few people making it across the border? If a Democrat mayor or governor stopped arresting and prosecuting criminals, would it mean that the crime rate went down? Just like fewer apprehensions at the border, or fewer criminal arrests and prosecutions would lead to greater numbers of incursions at our border and of crimes committed, suppressing the number of election fraud and voter fraud cases will logically result in more election fraud and voter fraud.

UNDERMINING ELECTION INTEGRITY

Democrats have pursued an "all of the above" long-term strategy to destroy election integrity. They are committed to fighting every effort to make elections more secure, and they fight ferociously for any measure that will make it easier for them to control election results. They are aided and abetted by activist judges and a complicit media that are all too willing to spread lies and false narratives. They have many tools in their election rigging and election fraud toolbox.

Dirty Voter Rolls

Judicial Watch and other groups concerned about election integrity have worked tirelessly through the courts to try to require states and local jurisdictions to clean up voter rolls. These efforts have been fought tooth and nail, and when Judicial Watch or others prevail, compliance does not necessarily follow. The problem is so egregious that some jurisdictions have significantly more registered voters on their voter rolls than there are voting age adults in their jurisdiction. The practice of Democrats maintaining dirty voter rolls has been a problem for many years, but the mailing of unsolicited ballots to all registered voters in the 2020 election cycle was disastrous for election integrity. This was one of the more brazen initiatives taken by Democrats in the 2020 election.

Motor-Voter Registration

Some states allow voter registration when people get their drivers licenses at the Department of Motor Vehicles. They use the argument that this makes it easier for people to get registered to vote, which is true, but the problem is that they are lax in verifying that individuals seeking to register to vote at the DMV are actually eligible to vote as United States citizens. In some states, it is as simple as checking a box that you would like to register to vote, and you become registered automatically. Making registering to vote easier makes it easier for people to vote illegally.

Same-Day Registration

Allowing people to register to vote on the day that an election is conducted is one of the methods by which Democrats pursue their "all of the above" strategy to undermine election integrity. There is no reason for states to allow people to register to vote on Election Day other than to undermine election integrity. It makes too much sense to close out the window for voter registration thirty days prior to an election in order to publish the complete list of eligible voters in the election. This looks too much like election integrity to be something that Democrats would accept.

Allowing same-day registration, like many of their other tactics and methods, is an artificial line drawn in the sand by Democrats. They will get on their moral high horses and vigorously defend the right of voters to register as late as possible as if it is a natural right given to us by our Creator, when in fact they are simply maximizing their opportunity to commit election fraud.

Absentee and Early Voting

Absentee voting and early voting have always been problematic in maintaining election integrity. It is difficult to maintain chain of custody on such ballots, as ballots bounce around the U.S. Postal Service and election offices. Too many hands touch these ballots to make absentee or early voting acceptable. Ballots could be discarded or switched at various points in the process.

Absentee voting and early voting create the circumstances where using centralized counting centers is almost unavoidable. You can't count such votes at the precinct where those votes would have normally been cast. The door is thrown open for centralized election fraud activities on a massive scale.

Ballot Harvesting

I don't know when ballot harvesting was introduced by Democrats as a method to stuff ballot boxes, but the first I learned of it was during the 2018 congressional races in California where Democrats flipped several historically Republican congressional seats. The practice of third parties going around gathering up absentee ballots from voters creates the opportunity for coercion, intimidation, bribery and the switching or discarding of ballots. There are serious chain-of-custody issues with this practice, and it should never be tolerated in an election.

Centralized Counting Centers

Whether by mistake or intentional fraud, counting centers have so many opportunities for potential election fraud to occur. The storage and handling of ballots and the use of electronic tabulation machines create the perfect opportunity for nefarious actors to steal elections. Democrats and unscrupulous Republicans or third-party actors have designed a system that virtually requires massive counting centers with wide open opportunities for fraud. Using complex ballots is just one way that they have used to create this problem.

Combining numerous decisions on a ballot creates the need to use electronic tabulation machines in centralized counting centers. One of the best illustrations of this problem occurred in the 2018 midterm elections in Broward County, Florida. Brenda Sykes became well known as the administrator of the counting center in Broward, where they seemed to misplace approximately 2500 ballots. At the time she said "they are here somewhere" after more than one recount that came up short. One possible explanation for the shortfall in ballots at the counting center is that approximately 2500 ballots were counted twice.

Using centralized counting centers creates huge problems for maintaining custody and control of the ballots. The centralization of the process also gives nefarious actors the opportunity to conduct election fraud on a massive scale with few witnesses.

Over-Voting

When it comes to voter turnout that is close to or exceeds the number of eligible people of voting age in certain election jurisdictions, it has been my observation that those impressive turnouts almost always happen in Democrat majority districts. Republicans have been tolerating these mathematically and statistically unlikely outcomes for too long.

Black-Box Voting

Voting electronically and electronic tabulation of votes is one of the most vulnerable areas of our election system where these methods are used because it is impossible for the average person to understand and observe the process from start to finish. This is why some countries absolutely forbid electronic voting or vote tabulation. The incremental undermining of election integrity has made "black-box voting" almost essential. This has been by design.

Bev Harris, author of *Black-Box Voting*, and Bennie Smith documented these risks years ago at her website, blackboxvoting.org, and in a video entitled *Fraction Magic*, which demonstrated the many vulnerabilities of machine voting and tabulation. The manipulation of electronic voting and tabulation is not limited to Democrats, as the nonpartisan efforts of Bev and Bennie revealed election fraud in Republican races. Their work should convince anyone desiring honest elections to reject electronic voting and the electronic tabulation of votes.

Crony Capitalism

The United States electoral system has long operated on a "pay to play" basis, where money has played too significant a role in who gets elected and who has access to elected officials once they are elected. Early in the process, most candidates bend the knee to the kingmakers, lobbyists, bundlers and major donors. Most elected officials are elected with a sense of indebtedness to the moneyed interests that they believe got them elected.

The problem starts on a small scale at the local and state level, but escalates to astounding proportion at the national level. There are recent examples that show how openly egregious crony capitalism manifests itself by those at the highest levels in the federal government. Was Solyndra a payoff by Obama to donors? Was there a quid pro quo involved with the hundreds of millions of dollars granted to a publisher to develop common core curriculum that then paid Obama $65 million for a book deal? Was the Clinton foundation a pay to play scheme that quickly dried up after Clinton lost her bid for president?

Would Hunter Biden have been able to secure his lucrative deals with companies from Ukraine, China and other countries if his father was not vice president? Is the artwork sold by Hunter Biden for exorbitant funds simply a payoff for the sale of access and influence with his dad? The list goes on and on.

The greatest threat that crony capitalism poses to United States sovereignty and economic prosperity is the systematic way that the

corrupt relationship between global corporations and elected officials has led to the selling out of United States citizens. There is too
much money sloshing around from big corporations that influence
elected officials to assist those corporations in building moats
around their monopolies and oligopolies.

Lawfare Tactics

Using litigation to undermine election integrity or to influence
outcomes in specific races is not something that Democrats enjoy a
monopoly on, but they ramped up their efforts after the 2016 election of Donald Trump. They were successful in states like Georgia,
where they persuaded the executive branch to enter into a secret
consent decree, which was rubberstamped by the judicial branch.
This effectively bypassed and undermined the plenary authority that
the Georgia legislature has over elections. They tried similar tactics
in Texas, but were unsuccessful.

Democrats are tenacious in their efforts, and they fight tooth
and nail to not give up any ground that they conquer through their
lawfare efforts. Where they can't get legislation they desire, they try
to effect change through the back door with the judiciary. Democrat efforts in this area had a profound effect on the 2020 election.

All of these practices have been used by Democrats to create
opportunities for election fraud for decades, but the 2020 election
cycle presented an opportunity for Democrats to employ these
methods at an unprecedented scale.

CAPITALIZING ON COVID-19

We can only hope that the truth will eventually win out over the lies
that have been perpetrated over Covid-19 and the 2020 election.
The fact that Covid-19 is serious and deadly is undisputed, but as I
write these words new revelations have come to light that perhaps
vindicate those that have had questions about the origin of Covid-
19, the necessity of masks or shutdowns, the efficacy of certain

therapeutics that were rejected previously, and the appropriateness and necessity of declaring Covid-19 a pandemic, declaring a state of emergency and approving vaccines on an emergency basis that have not been adequately tested.

Perhaps we will know the truth about these questions in due time, but it is abundantly clear that Covid-19 was used as a pretext to foist unprecedented changes to the election process upon us. Many believe that Covid-19 was used to get rid of President Donald Trump and to set the stage for the global elites to reset the global financial system. These elites themselves even refer to "The Great Reset" that they plan to implement.

The depth and breadth of the astounding and mind-numbing actions taken in the 2020 election by Democrats and their globalist puppet-masters is why I refer to the 2020 election as the "2020 election farce." Steve Bannon calls it "a wound that will not heal."

Mailing Unsolicited Ballots

The mailing of unsolicited ballots to all voters on the voter rolls of primarily Democrat-controlled election jurisdictions is one of the most egregious actions taken by Democrats in the 2020 election. Covid-19 was used as a justification for taking this unprecedented action. Not only did they send unsolicited absentee ballots to properly registered citizen voters, they included all of the dubious "voters" on their dirty voter rolls. Democrats resisted efforts to clean up voter rolls of dead voters or voters that had moved away, and they knowingly and shamefully mailed excess absentee ballots to them. What could possibly go wrong with such a scenario?

Ballot Drop-Boxes

In order to accommodate the huge surge in absentee ballots mailed out to voters, many jurisdictions decided to use ballot drop boxes for the collection of those ballots. This created significant chain of custody issues, and opened up more opportunities for mis-

chief by nefarious actors. Ballot boxes were also placed dispropor-
tionately in larger numbers in Democrat areas.

Violations of State Laws

There were many violations of state law in the 2020 election
that had significant impact on the results. The secret settlement
agreement entered into by the executive branch officials in the state
of Georgia circumvented the Georgia legislature. The unilateral
extension of time to count late ballots in the Commonwealth of
Pennsylvania was a violation of Pennsylvania law. In Wisconsin,
bureaucrats relaxed the definition of the indefinite confinement
requirement that voters had to meet in order to request absentee
ballots, which resulted in a surge of such requests.

Counting Late Ballots

One of the manifestations of the "count every vote" mantra by
Democrats is their push to count votes that arrive after deadlines
established by state law. This happened on a massive scale in the
Commonwealth of Pennsylvania, where Democrats in the executive
branch violated state law by accepting and counting votes that were
received after Election Day. Although the Supreme Court required
that such votes be separated and counted separately, Democrats
won by default on this issue because the Supreme Court later chose
not to get involved in a close examination of what happened during
the 2020 election.

Lack of Transparency

Instead of transparency, Democrats seek a complex, opaque
election system that makes it easy for them to commit fraud. There
have been serious transparency and accountability issues for a long
time, but the 2020 election was not transparent by design. The lack
of transparency continues even to the time of this writing in the
middle of 2021. Nefarious actors are resisting all efforts to get to

the truth because they know what the truth is. They obfuscate every step of the way in every state where We the People are trying to get to the truth.

Scott Adams, Dilbert creator, said it well when he said that the election in Wayne County Michigan was "not transparent by force." Workers in the centralized counting center prohibited Republican observers from being in the room, and they went so far as to cover up the windows. Why do that if they don't have something to hide?

Funding of Election Process by Outsiders

According to reports, many election jurisdictions accepted funding of the election process from outside third parties, but apparently it wasn't without strings attached. There are reports of Mark Zuckerberg or entities funded by him entering into contracts with election jurisdictions to provide resources to assist in accommodating changes to the 2020 election process with stipulations that, if not met, would require a refund of the resources provided.

Some of the unprecedented changes in the 2020 election created additional financial burdens upon election jurisdictions, so it was an open door for someone like Mark Zuckerberg to have undue influence on the process. It would take an examination of specific contracts and the actions of local authorities to fully appreciate the impact of outside funding, but some states have recognized the problem, and have introduced legislation banning the funding of election processes by third-party outsiders.

Lax Signature Verification

The huge increase in absentee ballots during the 2020 election, particularly unsolicited mail-in ballots that were sent to dirty voter rolls, created numerous problems. In addition to creating the opportunity to stuff ballot boxes with fraudulent votes, the magnitude of the increase in absentee ballots that had to be handled differently than ballots cast at voting precincts on Election Day made it difficult to maintain proper chain of custody over all of the ballots. It also made it virtually impossible to follow signature matching requirements set forth in state law.

Signature matching scanners were used with lower accuracy settings in order to dramatically reduce the number of rejected ballots that would have ordinarily occurred. State laws were violated, and the courts were generally lax in requiring election administrators to conform to state laws. One of the many reasons why the 2020 election was a total farce was the fact that ballot boxes were stuffed with questionable ballots, and every measure intended to assure election integrity was severely compromised.

Ceding Control of Election to Vendors

As of this writing, the Maricopa County Arizona forensic audit is in progress. One of the early revelations in the forensic audit was the fact that the administration of the election was not under the full and direct control of the election administrators responsible for the election. In Maricopa County and in many other election jurisdictions, the Dominion Voting Systems personnel seemed to be the go-to people during the election, and during the tabulation of votes in the centralized voting centers.

It was also discovered that the Maricopa County election officials were not in possession of the administrative passwords necessary for the forensic auditors to have full access to the voting or tabulation machines. If election integrity is a primary objective, it is a huge problem for election administrators to yield control of elections to vendors.

An examination of contracts between election administrators and vendors involved with the election process in their jurisdictions would likely reveal that there was a pattern throughout the country for election administrators to yield inappropriate control of the election process in their jurisdictions to those vendors. This should be unacceptable to any state seeking to assure election integrity.

Another significant area of concern is the fact that some election jurisdictions entered into contracts with vendors using electronic voting machines or electronic tabulation machines that used proprietary software systems that were not accessible and transparent to the election administrators or to anyone involved in an official forensic audit of the election results. Contracts such as these should never be entered into, as it guarantees that elections conducted under those contracts would not be transparent, and also make accurate audits next to impossible.

Election jurisdictions seeking to maximize election integrity should have never authorized the purchase of election systems that those jurisdictions would not have complete control over. Entering into contracts that require on-site or remote participation in the process by vendors is asking for trouble. Some of the activities of election officials in some states raise legitimate questions about the potential for corruption or compromise of those officials.

Using Ballot Images

Election jurisdictions have used high-speed centralized tabulation machines in prior elections, but the election process changes implemented for the 2020 election no doubt prompted greater use of high-speed centralized tabulation machines. We witnessed the rollout of massive centralized counting centers. One noteworthy revelation was that the tabulation of votes was conducted using ballot images rather than the actual ballots.

The Maricopa County forensic audit manually processed 2.1 million paper ballots that supposedly were all scanned with voting tabulation machines that created an image for each ballot and then tabulated all of the votes based upon those images. Rachel Maddow was rather panicked and excited that the forensic auditors actually had the paper ballots. As if it was some unfathomable development she exclaimed: "They have the ballots!" It is not some strange thing that We the People should expect the results of the forensic audit of actual paper ballots cast to match the results generated by the proprietary Dominion Voting Systems tabulation machines. Perhaps Rachel Maddow, the Maricopa County election administrators, Democrats and the Biden Regime Department of Justice already know the results that the audit will reveal, but the numbers of ballots cast and the tally of the votes are not the only data points that they have to worry about.

Adjudication of Ballots

One of the problems of using ballot images in the tabulation process is that when individual ballots are rejected from the system for one reason or another, they go into the adjudication process run by partisans. It has been demonstrated that the adjudication process involves sending ballots to individual adjudicators or judges that are supposed to have the wisdom to discern the intent of the voter.

We all remember the hanging chads and dimpled chads from the Florida recount in the 2000 presidential election. That process involved partisans from both parties observing the adjudication process while election administrators counted the ballots in question. The adjudication process in the 2020 election sent packets of ballots to individuals that were supposed to fairly and objectively decide the intent of voters without supervision by representatives of each of the two major parties.

Another problem with adjudicating ballot images is that those ballots, once adjudicated, would be placed into folders, and those folders could conveniently disappear. There is nothing that would stop nefarious actors from discarding ballots for one candidate in a folder and simply replacing those ballots with duplicates from another folder. These types of shenanigans come to mind when we hear about thumb drives discovered in drawers or disappearing altogether. Since everyone must be presumed to be a partisan in an election, sending packets of ballot images to individuals to decide the intent of voters is foolishness.

Dominion Voting Systems

The picture is developing quite clearly that Dominion Voting Systems is the "Grand Central Station" of the 2020 Election Farce. Their involvement in all of the contested states and other election jurisdictions representing approximately 35% of voters in the United States puts them front and center in the great controversy over the 2020 election that We the People must get to the bottom of. One thing that is crystal clear from the 2020 Election Farce is that we should never trust elections conducted using electronic voting or electronic tabulation machines, regardless of vendor.

Transition Integrity Project

In the summer of 2020, Democrats revealed their strategy for the 2020 Election Farce by publishing the Transition Integrity Project report. "Nonpartisans" had gamed out all of the scenarios and projected a win by Joe Biden after the dust settles. They did not advocate for election integrity in their documents, for they did not desire election integrity, but had already conspired to commit the greatest election fraud in United States history.

They were simply putting forth a strategy that would focus on the transition of power from the Trump administration to the Biden Regime. The partisan players participating in the Transition Integrity Project certainly showed no concern about the integrity of the transition of power from the Obama-Biden administration to the Trump administration back in 2017.

United States Postal Service

The 2020 Election Farce has conclusively proven that we should never trust the United States Postal Service to ever handle ballots again. There were instances where ballots were thrown away by postal workers. There are allegations that postal workers held up delivery of ballots. Whistleblowers from the USPS that came forward with evidence of wrongdoing were harassed and threatened.

Affidavits evidencing election fraud were signed under penalty of perjury, including one by a driver that states that he drove a trailer load of ballots from New York to Pennsylvania. Other affidavits reportedly assert that postal workers promised nefarious actors "a good handful" of ballots, and that there was a coordinated effort to backdate ballots received after Election Day.

There is simply too much evidence of wrongdoing to ever trust the United States Postal Service with our ballots again. It's a small matter, because we can cut the entire Gordian knot by implementing this plan to restore election integrity.

TWO

Restore Integrity to Federal Elections

WITHOUT ELECTION INTEGRITY, WE ARE NO LONGER GOVERNED BY THE CONSENT OF THE GOVERNED

Federal elections shall be held on the first Tuesday following the first Monday of November in even-numbered years, and no state or local election shall be held within sixty days of such Federal Election Day. Each citizen, having been lawfully registered to vote, shall personally present themselves to their assigned polling place on Election Day, with verifiable photographic identification, and shall affix their right thumbprint to a paper ballot, which shall be retained for one year.

– Proposed Constitutional Amendment Language

Designing federal elections with integrity should not be a difficult process. You would think that all Americans would be on the same page about conducting elections with integrity, but the truth is that there are many who are willing to cheat in order to win elections, and there are many that will turn a blind eye to those who cheat if the outcome is desirable to them. This book is not written to those people, as they have no interest in recognizing the truth about the lack of election integrity in the United States, and they are unwilling to permit We the People to restore election integrity.

This book is written for all United States citizens who value election integrity above election results, regardless of party. It is also written for freedom loving people around the world to use as a model for conducting fair and free elections with integrity in their home countries. Of all nations, the United States should be the gold standard of how elections should be run with transparency and accountability. How they should be run with integrity.

Everything starts with the design of the election process. An election system can be designed using technology where appropriate and very simple features that make the process very easy for observers to understand and monitor. We can have maximum integrity without sacrificing efficiency in the voting process, and without sacrificing speed and accuracy in the counting process.

The election process in the United States lacks integrity. It is a broken system, and most people know it. We arrived at where we are through the incremental chipping away of election integrity by nefarious actors that want to completely undermine election integrity so that they can control the results. We the People simply need to say enough is enough and get behind a plan to immediately restore integrity to federal elections. It's a simple plan, but not an easy one to implement because of the resistance we will see.

CITIZENSHIP AND BORDERS

Without election integrity, the United States is a banana republic, and its citizens are no longer governed by the consent of the governed. Likewise, without secure borders the United States is no longer a sovereign nation. The federal government has failed to fulfill its obligation to protect the states from invasion mandated by Article IV Section 4 of the Constitution.

The mission to restore election integrity begins with securing our borders from the invasion of illegal people and goods that Democrats have invited at an unprecedented level. We must immediately secure our borders and we must also immediately implement a system to verify the status of any person within our borders.

Our government maintains massive amounts of information on United States citizens. We the People should challenge the overreach of the federal government in this area, but we should embrace the idea of maintaining a database of vital statistics that will make it very easy to verify the legal status of any individual here, and thereby also easy to verify the eligibility of United States citizens to vote in the state of their declared residence.

With all that is going on in the world today with the prospect of vaccine passports, embedded chips and social credit scores, and talk of The Great Reset, we can plainly see how Bible prophecy that was written thousands of years ago is coming to be. We can see how easily a system could be implemented where people would not be able to buy or sell without the mark of the beast. God has given us biometric means by which we can identify ourselves without accepting electronic leashes.

We can fight over how much data the government collects and retains about each of us, but at this point we should be willing to accept the use of fingerprints for confirming our identity, our legal status, and our eligibility to vote in the state of our declared residence. In order to be accountable for income tax purposes we must declare a state of residence. In order for United States citizens to vote, we must declare a residential address that conforms to nexus requirements for that state of residence. Declaring a state of residency is also important for the census every ten years.

Libertarians may object to requiring people to declare a state of residency at all, and there are arguments about whether you should have to live in a state for six months to declare that state as your residence. Other than acknowledging that, in today's world of great mobility, people should have much more flexibility in how they qualify for residency for taxation and voting purposes, we will leave nuances like those to sort out at another time with appropriate state and federal legislation.

The Constitution grants Congress the authority to define United States citizenship, but the lack of enforcement of United States immigration law and the open border policies have created a crisis over our national sovereignty and the very essence of United States citizenship. Democrats and RINO Republicans have diluted the value of United States citizenship and the integrity of our elections. It is time that We the People demand that these problems be addressed so that we may restore the distinction and value of United States citizenship.

By implementing a very limited database that uses fingerprints, or other biometric data for those that don't have fingers, we can quickly sort out the legal status of any individual. Citizens that present themselves to election polling locations could quickly be confirmed as eligible, and the legal status of noncitizens could quickly be established. Noncitizens are either in the United States legally or illegally. Lax enforcement of immigration law has created a very complicated situation. Americans are compassionate people, but we also believe in the rule of law and in our national sovereignty.

We the People should demand that our border be immediately secured by all means available to us, and require that noncitizens present themselves for identification purposes so that we may establish the legal status of each individual. After a specified deadline, noncitizens that do not present themselves for identification purposes, or who do not periodically reconfirm their whereabouts could be subject to immediate deportation.

There are many complicated situations with immigration that have been created by lax and destructive policy, but with secure borders and this kind of a plan being implemented, Americans will patiently and compassionately accept the results of working through this process. Implementing this method of using fingerprints to identify the status of individuals will become a critical element of assuring the integrity of elections.

What is not acceptable to many Americans is for Democrats, RINO Republicans, and global elites to continue to destroy United States sovereignty and undermine the integrity of elections in this country. We the People must overcome our natural resistance to using fingerprints for identification purposes in order to assure the integrity of elections.

CENSUS AND REDISTRICTING

The census process every ten years has been used primarily by Democrats to manipulate the allocation of congressional seats and the share of federal dollars allocated to cities and states for federal programs and activities that fall outside of the enumerated powers granted to the federal government by the Constitution.

Establishing a federal database of vital statistics of persons in the United States will allow us to bring the census process every ten years into the 21st-century. We should debate the issue of whether or not to count noncitizens or illegal persons in the census totals that impact the apportionment of congressional seats, but there should be no real debate about the efficiency of conducting the census by simply counting those included in a federal vital statistics database that is continuously updated.

USING FINGERPRINTS FOR VOTING

To assure the greatest level of integrity in federal elections, each voter should affix their right thumbprint to the back of each ballot. Matching the identity of the voter by the thumbprint on the back of the ballot with the vote cast by the voter on the front of the ballot should be a felony under federal law that is punishable with severe consequences. It should be relatively easy to design a process that preserves the secret ballot.

Although it is theoretically possible for the voter on a particular ballot to be identified, it would be much easier to assure voter anonymity with this system than it would be under the current system. If there is a need to scan the fingerprints on the back of ballots in a voting precinct in order to verify that the ballots in hand were cast by people who were verified to be eligible to vote in that precinct, and actually voted at the precinct, great care could be taken to randomize the ballots prior to scanning only the fingerprints on the back of the ballots. If one or more fingerprints did not match valid voters, or if it was discovered that someone voted in more than one election jurisdiction, the back of the ballots could then be rescanned in order to isolate the suspect ballots.

Absolutely anything is possible with electronic voting, including violating the secret ballot. The use of mail-in voting, absentee voting, and early voting all present very significant opportunities for bad actors to violate secret ballot integrity. Dishonest people will find a way to violate election integrity, so the best we can do is work to absolutely minimize the possibilities for fraud, and impose severe penalties for election law violations. Many will object to affixing thumbprints or fingerprints to the back of ballots, but it offers the best balance of maximizing election integrity while maintaining our tradition of protecting the secret ballot.

One huge advantage of using fingerprints on the back of ballots is that there is virtually no way that fraudulent ballots could be inserted into the process. A ballot is only valid if it has a fingerprint on the back that matches an eligible voter. Plain paper ballots could be provided to each precinct in sufficient quantity to cover all of the voters of record that were properly registered to vote in that precinct 30 days prior to the federal election. Since only ballots with fingerprints of voters cleared through the check in process at the precinct would be valid, all other unused ballots would be useless. Without fingerprints on the back of each ballot and the ability to audit and confirm the authenticity of paper ballots held in storage for a year, the opportunity for election fraud would still be too great for We the People to tolerate.

REGISTRATION OF ELIGIBLE VOTERS

Each United States citizen should be required to establish eligibility and register to vote in a particular election jurisdiction thirty days prior to a federal election. United States citizenship will be easily confirmed by the individual's fingerprints matching with the federal database with the minimum vital statistics needed. Local election jurisdictions would be tied into the federal database so that the registration of that person in that election jurisdiction would automatically cancel any other prior registration in another election jurisdiction. The reconciliation of the federal database with local election jurisdictions will essentially force those election jurisdictions to keep their voter rolls clean and up to date.

At the close of business thirty days prior to the federal election, each local election jurisdiction should be required to publish the full list of all eligible voters in that election jurisdiction. In order for a voter to be eligible, they must have declared an address of residence in that election jurisdiction. If someone is homeless, that election jurisdiction could accommodate that person by whatever means is legally established in accordance with federal law. Homeless people should have the liberty to claim residency status for tax purposes and eligibility to vote in jurisdictions where they spend most of their time, but election jurisdictions should not be free to claim transient people as eligible voters, or to count them in the census.

All elections are locally administered, and voters have the right to challenge the eligibility of any person that claims to be eligible to vote in their jurisdiction. Confirming the right of citizens to question the legal status or residency of people on voter rolls is not voter intimidation, it is simply plain common sense. From billionaires to the homeless, voters have the right to know the residence of record of anyone who votes in any election. A billionaire that doesn't want to reveal an address has the liberty to not vote, but has no right to vote anonymously. What is critical is that we eliminate the possibility for people to vote in more than one jurisdiction in any particular election.

Thirty days is sufficient time for voters in an election jurisdiction to vet each other and make sure that there are no shenanigans, such as voters registered to vacant lots or public buildings, or dozens of voters registered to an apartment. Voters also have a right to know the names and addresses of all eligible voters so that they may campaign for their candidate of choice.

Each election jurisdiction should likewise be required to publish the full list of actual voters that voted in the election, and there should not be any additional voters that were not on the list of registered voters published thirty days prior to the election. The practice of some election jurisdictions of producing more actual votes than there were registered voters needs to come to an end.

DECOUPLE FEDERAL ELECTIONS FROM STATE AND LOCAL ELECTIONS

The first order of business in restoring election integrity is to decouple federal elections from state and local elections. Elections have become so complex because there are so many decisions on ballots that voting electronically or scanning and counting ballots electronically is required. Nefarious actors have capitalized on this weakness in our election system. The doors have been thrown open to innumerable methods of committing election fraud, and because there are so many decisions being made on one ballot it is more difficult for voters to be informed about each decision.

The need for electronic voting and electronic tabulation of votes can be eliminated by simplifying the federal election process by prohibiting the combination of any state or local election with federal elections. There are normally three or fewer decisions made by voters in an election jurisdiction in a federal election. When we decouple federal elections from state and local elections, we will be able to conduct the federal election in each jurisdiction with a paper ballot for each decision that can be easily sorted and counted at each precinct within hours after the polls close.

By using high-tech methods when appropriate and low-tech methods when appropriate, we can restore election integrity. All of the nefarious actors will fight tooth and nail to keep us from doing this, but We the People should demand that we decouple federal elections from state and local elections so that we can have fair and accurate federal elections, setting an example for states to do likewise. Most states would hold their elections in odd numbered years, and states seeking election integrity will decouple statewide elections from local elections and implement paper ballots for each decision that can be sorted and counted immediately after polls close.

LIMIT ABSENTEE VOTING

The opportunities for voter fraud and election fraud are too great for We the People to tolerate early voting in any form. Of all of the methods nefarious actors have used to undermine election integrity, expanding the time period during which people can vote from a single day to numerous days and sometimes weeks has been one of the most destructive. We must return to holding federal elections on a single day.

Absentee voting should be limited to very few exceptions, and even with those exceptions, all absentee ballots should be cast on Election Day at authorized polling locations that will then forward absentee ballots cast to a state election office by secure courier. The state election office will then sort the absentee ballots by state, and then send those ballots to each of the other state election offices by secure courier. State election offices would then forward ballots to congressional districts. The 2020 election proved that we cannot trust the United States Postal Service to handle ballots in any way.

Military personnel and those serving in United States embassies and similar roles should be permitted to vote absentee on Election Day at polling locations established on those installations. Each voter would still be required to properly register at their local election jurisdiction, and would use ballots sent to them by their election jurisdiction. Congress could approve limited essential occupations that could be granted the right to cast absentee ballots, but those ballots would be cast at authorized polling locations, and those polling locations would forward those ballots to state election offices charged with the responsibility of delivering absentee ballots to each congressional district.

In all cases, each absentee voter would affix his fingerprint to the back of each ballot in the presence of authorized poll administrators before the voter enters a voting booth, casts his ballots, and inserts his ballots into an envelope with a preprinted label identifying the state and congressional district for which the ballots are cast. That envelope could be sealed, and the voter could affix his thumbprint to the outside of that envelope for the authorized polling location to forward to the appropriate congressional district.

Election results would be known within hours of polls closing. In addition to reporting the votes cast for each candidate for each office by voters in that precinct, each precinct would also report the number of absentee ballots cast by congressional district that it is forwarding to the appropriate congressional districts through the process prescribed by Congress. The name of each absentee voter would be provided, and those names should be known by and duly noted by each election jurisdiction. There should be no surprises, and no shifting totals of uncounted ballots.

VOTE BY PAPER BALLOTS ONLY

If We the People are to restore election integrity, it is critical that we demand that federal elections only be conducted using paper ballots, and that fingerprints are affixed to the back of each ballot. We can use a combination of high-tech methods to maintain a current list of eligible voters and their biometric information that local election jurisdictions can use to properly register voters and to verify their identification at the polling location on the day of the election, coupled with the low-tech option of using paper ballots for each decision that a voter makes.

Since a federal election normally has a maximum of three decisions to be made, white paper could be used for the congressional race, light blue paper could be used for the presidential race, and light red or pink paper could be used for the Senate race. This will make the sorting of ballots easier and more transparent.

By decoupling federal elections from state and local elections, using paper ballots for each decision made by voters, and limiting the size of each election precinct, federal elections can be conducted quickly and accurately with the highest level of integrity possible. The results of the federal election can be known with certainty within hours after the polls close.

VOTING ON FEDERAL ELECTION DAY

This plan to restore election integrity is simple, but not easy. If We the People are successful in restoring election integrity, Federal Election Day will be a great celebration, and it will go smoothly and the results will be accurate and quickly known.

The population serviced by each election precinct established by states should be limited by federal law or constitutional amendment. If Congress were to use a limit of the population size of 5000, then a congressional district of approximately 750,000 people could have as few as 150 election precincts.

When each voter shows up at their polling location they will have been properly registered and certified to be eligible to vote in that election jurisdiction thirty days prior to Federal Election Day. They will have provided their thumbprint or fingerprints in order to assure the greatest level of election integrity as well as to make the process go quickly and efficiently.

The average voter shouldn't have to wait long to vote, and when they get to the check-in table they will simply scan their thumbprint and their picture and voter eligibility and registration information will show up on the screen of the person checking them in. Partisan observers could verify the identity of the voter, and perhaps the public voter information would flash on a screen for the public to observe. After all, the information was publicly available for thirty days for other voters in the election precinct to challenge if they wanted to, or to campaign for the vote of that voter for a particular candidate.

After his identity and eligibility is verified, the voter steps to the next station, where he receives a ballot for each race to be decided in the election. He receives a white ballot for the congressional race. He receives a light blue ballot for the presidential race, if there is one. He receives a pink ballot for the Senate race, if there is one.

The voter then places his right thumbprint on the upper right corner of the back of each ballot and wipes his thumb off with a tissue provided by the poll worker. The indelible ink residue on his thumb makes a great substitute for the "I Voted" stickers. At this point the voter might be given a 6 x 9 manila envelope with enough holes in it, that when the poll worker holds it up, it will demonstrate to witnesses and live stream video that nothing is in the envelope. The envelope could then be used by the voter to insert the folded ballots into, after he marks his ballots in the voting booth.

The voter then goes into the voting booth with his ballots, marks them and folds them in half. If given a manila envelope, the voter inserts his folded ballots into the manila envelope. When the voter exits the voting booth he would then hold his manila envelope up for people to see that there are indeed ballots inside the manila envelope, and he would then drop his manila envelope into a large Plexiglas ballot box.

If no manila envelope is used, the voter would exit the voting booth and either drop all three folded ballots into a large Plexiglas ballot box, or drop each ballot of different colors into Plexiglas ballot boxes designated for each of those colors. The voter then smiles for the cameras, grateful for the transparent election process that he is participating in, and exits the voting area.

ASSISTED VOTING

Exceptions to this procedure for people that don't have a right thumb or any other digits with fingerprints, or blind voters, etc. would all be worked out. A feisty old grandma that needs assistance in voting, but who does not want her woke grandson to change her intended vote in the voting booth should have the option to give up her right to a secret ballot by verbalizing her intent publicly and on live stream so that someone could assist her in marking her ballots as she states her intent. Not everyone is paranoid about maintaining the secrecy of their vote, so in a complex situation a voter should have the right to openly declare their vote, and have someone publicly mark their ballot for them.

In order to assist the elderly in voting on Federal Election Day, polling locations could be established at nursing homes with all of the protocols for transparency in place. Such a polling location might be an official precinct polling location where other members of the local precinct would vote, or nursing homes could be set up as polling locations for absentee ballots cast in the same manner as military bases or embassies. Under all circumstances, residents of nursing homes who vote must show up at the polling location and demonstrate that they have the cognitive ability to vote, and they must be able to cast their vote without influence. The elderly and infirm are especially vulnerable to coercion and intimidation, and we must protect them and the election process from abuse.

SIMULTANEOUS VOTING ACROSS NATION

It would be very beneficial if we aligned voting hours across the nation. Voting hours on Federal Election Day could be 9 AM to 9 PM Eastern time, 8 AM to 8 PM Central time, 7 AM to 7 PM Mountain time, 6 AM to 6 PM Pacific time, 5 AM to 5 PM Alaska time, and 4 AM to 4 PM Hawaii and Aleutian time.

In this scenario all polls would close at the same time, and results of the federal election should be known within a couple of hours. This would limit the opportunity for the suppression of votes in Western time zones based upon Eastern Time zone results, and we would be united as a nation in real time voting and watching the results. At a minimum, the continental United States should all be voting in the same twelve hour period.

35

FEDERAL HOLIDAY AND CELEBRATION

We the People may choose to keep our federal elections on the first Tuesday after the first Monday in November in even-numbered years, but we should consider making Federal Election Day a national holiday. If we make it a holiday, we may want to change Federal Election Day to a Monday or a Friday. In any event, Federal Election Day should be a day of celebrating our Republic, our Constitution, our liberty, and our special obligation to promote liberty and resist tyranny throughout the world. When We the People are successful in restoring election integrity and saving our Republic, we should always celebrate Federal Election Day as deliverance from tyranny, socialism, and oppression.

ELECTION TRANSPARENCY

Elections with integrity will be conducted with the highest level of transparency. We the People must be able to understand and observe every step in the process in order to have confidence in our elections. We must eliminate every conceivable means by which election fraud and voter fraud can be committed by the nefarious actors that will do so if they are able. We must put sufficient barriers in place that we keep honest people honest, and we must have severe penalties for those who violate the most sacred civil institution that a society can have.

Leading up to an election, voter rolls are meticulously updated and made public. The list of actual voters is reported as soon as practicable after the polls close. Real-time reporting of who has actually voted must not happen so that voter intimidation and harassment will not take place while the polls are open.

Each polling location can be set up with a perimeter area for the general public to observe the process in an orderly manner. The intimidation or harassment of voters must not be tolerated. The entire process should be live streamed, and observers should be permitted to also live stream the process from their perspective.

After polls close, the sorting and counting of ballots must also be live streamed and observable.

One benefit of maximum transparency is that We the People will be able to see bad actors in action. Bad actors can then be held accountable by their opponents, and also by honest, fair-minded people within their own party. We the People will be able to easily identify bad actors, as they will fight tooth and nail to stop or water down this plan to restore election integrity.

COUNTING, REPORTING AND STORAGE OF BALLOTS

After polls close, ballots are moved to counting tables adjacent to the polling booths, or if space is limited, the polling booths are removed and the counting tables set up. Ballots are sorted by office, white ballots for the congressional race go to one table, and if there is a Senate or presidential race, those ballots go to counting tables for those races. A small precinct might use one counting table and count each race separately.

The ballots for each race should be sorted into stacks by the candidate voted for. Ballots for each candidate should be counted and binder clipped into stacks of 100, with the residual votes clipped into stacks of ten for easy counting. This simple counting process is just like what the British did with the Brexit referendum. All of the counts could be double-checked and triple-checked by partisans seeking to assure accuracy and integrity. Once there is consensus, results should be reported publicly, and to the election office to which the precinct reports.

Once the counting of ballots has been completed and reported, it is important that the ballots for each precinct be stored in storage boxes identifying which precinct they belong to and stored in a common congressional district storage facility with all of the other ballots from all of the other precincts in the congressional district. At this point in the process there should be absolute integrity in the results reported, but the ballots must be preserved in the event an audit or recount is required for a particular precinct or the entire congressional district.

With a maximum of three races, the ballots for each race for each precinct could be stored in three separate storage boxes about the size of a case of paper. With about 150 to 250 precincts in a congressional district, and a maximum of three storage boxes for each precinct, the 450 to 750 storage boxes could easily be stored in a fairly small facility with a counting area to be used as needed for a recount or audit. After a year, the ballots should be shredded and incinerated or shredded and turned into pulp for recycling so that there is no possibility of nefarious actors matching the fingerprints to the actual votes cast. The storage facility would then be prepared to receive the ballots from the next federal election.

REQUIRE STATE LEGISLATURES TO MEET TO CERTIFY FEDERAL ELECTION RESULTS

After observing what happened during the 2020 Election Farce, we must recognize that by federal statute, constitutional amendment, or state statute, state legislatures must convene to certify that the results reported in the federal election were in accordance with state and federal election law. We the People must hold our state legislatures accountable to fulfilling their obligation that elections be conducted in accordance with state and federal law. States must not permit overreach by the executive or judicial branches to subvert election integrity.

We the People must demand that our legislatures certify that a full and complete list of all eligible registered voters was made public thirty days prior to Federal Election Day, and voters on that list were United States citizens eligible to vote as residents of their state. We must also demand that they certify that a full and complete list of all of the eligible voters that actually voted was published as soon as practicable after the polls closed on Federal Election Day.

We the People must demand that our state legislatures certify that each federal election was conducted fairly, accurately, and with full transparency. We must demand that if our state legislatures cannot make such a certification of a federal election, that a new election would be immediately scheduled, and that all deficiencies in the prior election are corrected.

CAMPAIGN FINANCE AND REPORTING

The current FEC regulations regarding financial reporting for campaigns is onerous for some candidates, and lacking in transparency for well-funded and well organized campaigns. We can use twenty-first century technology to provide real-time reporting of campaign contributions and campaign expenditures in a manner that provides full transparency for the big money campaigns but also makes it very easy for first-time candidates with little financial and accounting support to wage an effective campaign.

Campaign finance laws should be modified to require that all campaign contributions accepted by campaigns be immediately made visible on public platforms, and that all expenditures would likewise be visible on the same platform once payments are made. There are numerous cloud-based accounting systems that could be modified slightly to make deposits and expenditures immediately available to the public.

This kind of transparency would make it unnecessary for campaigns to provide quarterly reports to the FEC, as the information would be available publicly in real time. Such systems may not exist at the moment, but with legislation requiring it as of two years after the legislation is passed, existing accounting platforms would quickly spin off competing solutions that would do the job.

Not only would such a system make it easier for first-time candidates to run for office without going afoul of federal election law, it would provide the opportunity for instant scrutiny of campaign contributions by citizen watchdogs. Contributions received by a campaign from a questionable source that creates a public uproar could permit the campaign to quickly reverse the transaction and refuse the funds from the questionable contributor.

In addition to real-time, online reporting of campaign contributions and expenditures, campaign finance laws should be modified to limit campaign contributions to contributions from natural persons that are United States citizens. There should also be no limitation on contributions from United States citizens. Such legislation would prohibit contributions from entities such as corporations and political action committees.

These two changes would bring much-needed transparency to campaign financing and reporting. It would eliminate dark money and bring all of the money directed to campaigns into the light.

Designing an election system with integrity should be a fairly simple process. Implementing such a design requires that participants are committed to maximizing election integrity, with the secondary goal of generating accurate results as quickly as possible. It is incumbent upon We the People to see to it that our broken election system is replaced with common sense procedures, systems, and controls that handle the logistics of federal elections efficiently, accurately, and transparently.

THREE

Show Me the Evidence!

THOSE WHO SEE NO EVIDENCE OF 2020 ELECTION FRAUD ARE WILLFULLY BLIND

There is none so blind as those who will not see.

– John Heywood

People that deny that there is ample evidence to demonstrate that the 2020 election was completely fraudulent are either part of the problem or they simply haven't opened their eyes to look. They are uninformed or are simply lying to themselves or lying to others. Democrats have made steady encroachments upon election integrity for decades, and spineless Republicans let them get away with it. Covid-19 was used as an excuse to pull out all the stops on committing election fraud on a massive scale.

EVIDENCE FOR THOSE WILLING TO SEE

For millions of Americans, the evidence of massive election fraud perpetrated by nefarious actors coordinating their activities to steal the 2020 election is obvious and overwhelming. We see compelling evidence that we believe warrants a thorough investigation and full forensic audit in order to establish all of the facts.

The primary purpose of this book is to articulate a simple plan to restore election integrity, not to prove something to those who are unwilling to even consider evidence of election fraud. I think it is useful to present some of the evidence that we know so far, for those honest enough to recognize that there is a problem with election integrity in this country, and who perhaps might be willing to get to the bottom of it and work with us to fix the problem.

Suppression of Evidence

There has been a concerted effort on the part of thousands of people collaborating to suppress evidence that is out in the open for everyone to see. The very suppression of evidence is evidence of the problem. Why would people be so fearful of examining the truth if the truth was not going to prove the fraud? They are simply afraid of the truth being known. Truth seekers have been denied almost every opportunity to present evidence in courts of law. Courts are complicit in the suppression of evidence because most courts have refused to hear cases on the merits, but have rather found lame excuses not to examine evidence that is available for objective evaluation.

We the People have seen too much evidence to allow the 2020 Election Farce to stand unchallenged. An army of truth seekers is rising up to take on those who would deprive our nation of fair and just elections. The system is irredeemably broken, but those who are part of the problem, whether through willful deed or ignorance, claim that we actually do have election integrity. If they are correct they should not fear the absolute truth being known to all. They prove our case by suppressing evidence and by refusing measures designed to assure election integrity.

One of the most compelling pieces of evidence of the fraud involved in the 2020 Election Farce, and the fraud in prior elections is the resistance by the left of the adoption of a simple plan that will guarantee election integrity in federal elections. Democrats are pushing an "all of the above" strategy to institutionalize election fraud, and We the People must push back with an "all of the above" strategy to impose election integrity on all fifty states.

Navarro Report

Peter Navarro has published a three part report that presents numerous categories of potentially illegal votes in the six battleground states that were hotly contested on the night of the election,

November 3, 2020. The fair-minded person that reads the Navarro Report should easily see that there is an abundance of evidence that can be brought out into the open to prove or disprove election fraud. The fact of the matter is that we will never be able to know the full truth, because so many illegal ballots have been intermingled that we will never be able to distinguish from legal ballots.

The Navarro report asserts that there are certain numbers of ballots in several categories that are potentially illegal, and compares the total of those potentially illegal ballots to the margin of victory that Joe Biden supposedly won by in each state. The Navarro report shows a pattern of fraudulent activity across the six battleground states examined in the report, but it also indicates that the pattern of election fraud most likely impacted many other states.

Mike Lindell

Mike Lindell has been focused on proving that the machine results recorded in the 2020 presidential race were fraudulent. He has produced several videos that would be worthwhile watching for anyone who is interested in seeking out the truth of what actually happened in the 2020 election.

Lindell gets into some of the same categories and numbers of potentially illegal ballots that Peter Navarro detailed in the Navarro report, but what I found most fascinating is the presentation Mike Lindell makes about how "white hat" hackers captured all of the "P-Caps," or "packet captures" of election information being transferred over the internet.

These packet captures will be presented by Lindell at a meeting he is hosting in South Dakota to cybersecurity experts invited to examine the packets for authenticity and for the conclusions that Lindell claims will prove election fraud and the extent and magnitude of that fraud. Evidently the packet captures contain unalterable information about the tabulation of votes, and the potential altering of votes. The mere existence of packet captures is a problem.

Rudy Giuliani

When adversaries have a hard time attacking the truth of the message, they usually attack the messenger, which is why personal attacks against Rudy Giuliani, known as "America's Mayor," indicate that Rudy has been over the target with the truth. Before serving as one of the best mayors in New York City in a century, Rudy took down the five mafia families in New York, as well as corrupt Wall Street criminals. He is tenacious in collecting and presenting evidence, and We the People can trust him to get to the truth.

It is astounding to me how resistant the Department of Justice, the FBI, and the courts have been to considering compelling evidence that Rudy has made available to them. Nevertheless, Rudy made presentations to state legislators when they were willing to consider the evidence that he had, and he continues to make every effort to discover new evidence, and to inform patriots of the evidence he has uncovered.

People have given Rudy evidence because they know that he can be trusted with that evidence. When the FBI failed to do anything with the Hunter Biden laptop, the technician that originally turned it over to the FBI provided a copy to Rudy. The FBI and other law enforcement agencies did nothing when Rudy brought the laptop to their attention, and when the FBI raided Rudy's home in a political investigation by the Southern District of New York, they took everything but copies of Hunter Biden's hard drive.

The Democrats overplayed their hand in the 2020 Election Farce, and people like Peter Navarro, Mike Lindell, Rudy Giuliani and thousands of others will not rest until the great fraud of the 2020 election is exposed and the wound healed by restoring election integrity throughout our country.

"Glitches" in Tabulation Software

Antrim County, Michigan experienced what was described as "glitches" in their electronic tabulation of votes. The "glitch" was

44

ascribed to human error, but I think it has clearly been proven that it was a problem with the electronic tabulation not matching with a hand count. I think the human error was made by someone committing fraud that was exposed. Similar problems were discovered in other election jurisdictions, and I'm sure that if the truth were known, that the entire system of electronically tabulating votes is corrupt, and will not match actual legal ballots cast.

To a fair and honest observer, I believe that what happened in Antrim County is clear evidence of election fraud. I believe the Democrats have been very careful to cover their tracks, but they are not perfect, and the hound dogs that are pursuing the rabbit trails of fraud will uncover more and more of what actually happened, hopefully to the point that minor players in the scheme will start turning state's evidence. My biggest concern is that the fraudsters will succeed in squashing the pursuit of the truth because they have control over the federal government, many of the election jurisdictions involved, and the media.

Late Night Shenanigans

Recorded surveillance video in Georgia revealed that cases of ballots were removed from under tables at a counting center in Fulton County. These ballots were counted in the middle of the night, after Republican observers were told that counting would not continue until the morning, and they were sent home. It is reasonable to assume that fraudulent ballots were being inserted into the count, which could explain why in multiple states there was a spike of ballots for Joe Biden in the middle of the night.

The fact that multiple hotly contested states almost simultaneously shut down counting of ballots indicates a coordinated action. The fact that multiple states could not give accurate guidance on exactly how many ballots were left to be counted throughout the counting process seems to show coordinated action. The entire election process in the 2020 Election Farce was riddled with a pattern of coordinated action that supports the notion that nefarious actors were coordinating their efforts to commit election fraud. People scoff at conspiracy theories, but a conspiracy is simply two or more people or entities coordinating their efforts to cause harm to another person, or entity. Conspiracies happen all the time. They aren't just theories to scoff at or dismiss.

Printing of Ballots

Complex ballots that are intended to be counted by high-speed electronic tabulation equipment require precise printing specifications that require a limited number of approved printers to complete the task of printing ballots. There is also the issue of maintaining proper controls in order to minimize the risk of counterfeit ballots being printed and inserted into the tabulation process. The fact that fraudulent ballots injected into the system under current use would be indistinguishable from legitimate ballots should require that special controls be built into the election process.

Ballots used in high-speed tabulation equipment have black squares or rectangles along the left edge of the ballot in order to assure alignment of the ballot so that optical scanners can properly pick up the votes cast for specific candidates. Ballots have been discovered that have rectangles or squares of different sizes in locations on the ballot that would have caused the rejection of those ballots in the tabulation process, which would send the ballot images to adjudication for people to judge who the votes were cast for.

It is alleged that such ballots with alignment issues were intentionally printed and intentionally delivered to Republican leaning election jurisdictions so that there would be a higher rate of rejected ballots requiring adjudication.

Counterfeit Ballots

One of the features of the Maricopa County, Arizona forensic audit is the examination of ballots that could perhaps be counterfeit

46

ballots. Absentee ballots should have been folded prior to mailing to voters and upon the return of those ballots by the voter. Ballots in Maricopa County, or in any election jurisdiction in the country that used absentee ballots, could be examined forensically to see whether or not the ballots were folded. Absentee ballots that were never folded would be fraudulent ballots.

Ballots that can be proven to have been marked by machine, and not by humans, are fraudulent, counterfeit ballots. One might wonder why nefarious actors would not take the time to hand mark and fold fraudulent ballots, but doing so on such a massive scale would require too many people to get the job done, hence too many potential witnesses or whistleblowers. A forensic analysis of the paper used for paper ballots under examination could potentially reveal counterfeit ballots based upon watermarks, fiber content, weight, and color of the paper.

Many affidavits have been signed by election process witnesses that alleged that ballots appeared to be pristine, unfolded, marked by machine, printed on inconsistent paper, or were cast in consecutive order for Joe Biden in such unrealistic percentages that it seemed improbable, if not impossible. The report of almost 100% of the ballots in a batch of 950 Georgia military absentee ballots being cast for Joe Biden is an example of such improbability.

Ballots Received Prior to Mailing

Curiously, numerous absentee ballots were recorded as having been received by election jurisdictions prior to the date of mailing of such ballots. Election jurisdictions should certainly have a record of when an absentee ballot was mailed to or given to a voter, and they should also record when those ballots were received back by the election jurisdiction. This data is simply part of a good control system over the process. There may be other explanations for how this could happen, but perhaps the most plausible explanation is that human error occurred when nefarious actors were making changes to voter databases in order to create counterfeit ballots for people that perhaps had not voted at all.

People committing crimes routinely leave forensic evidence of their crimes to be discovered by proper investigations. The problem with the 2020 Election Farce is that the perpetrators of the fraud, election officials, the courts, and mainstream media are all committed to denying a proper examination of the evidence that is there.

Statistical Analysis

People that say "show me the evidence" regarding the 2020 Election Farce without a genuine interest in seeking the truth and fleshing out the facts of the matter are the same people that say "follow the science" without being willing to take a scientific approach. These people have no interest in looking at something like statistical analysis to identify anomalies in election results.

Hillary Clinton won seven out of seven tossup decisions to decide who got delegates between her and Bernie Sanders in the 2016 Democrat primary. The mere fact that Hillary won seven out of seven does not prove that there was fraud, but since there is less than a 1% chance of this happening, it is reasonable to assume that fraud did in fact occur. Unless there was video evidence and testimony by numerous witnesses that a coin flip happened to come up for Hillary seven times straight, I choose to believe she won those contests by fraud. That is my informed belief.

Without getting bogged down in the body of statistical evidence that supports the notion that the 2020 Election Farce was indeed fraudulent, we can judge the aversion that Democrats have to the whole notion of statistical analysis as evidence that they know fraud happened and that they are fearful of that truth coming out.

The entire election system in the United States is irredeemably broken and is a complete farce. Election jurisdictions should publish the universe of eligible voters for their jurisdictions thirty days prior to every election, but they don't. They should publish the list of actual voters in each election as soon as possible after the election, but they don't.

If each election jurisdiction published the list of eligible voters, the list of actual voters that voted, and the actual number of people of voting age in their jurisdiction, we could compare those numbers to other election jurisdictions and probably see a pattern emerge of Democrat election jurisdictions massively outperforming Republican jurisdictions in terms of voter turnout. A little bit of statistical analysis would show this trend. Democrat jurisdictions have dirty voter rolls and they stuff the ballot boxes with fraudulent votes, and that can be proven beyond a shadow of a doubt by statistical analysis. The fact of the matter is that Democrats fear the truth, because they know they don't win elections fairly and honestly.

Censorship

Just as the suppression of evidence and the resistance to the implementation of reasonable measures to assure election integrity, the escalating blatant censorship of those who question the integrity of the 2020 election is evidence that something is seriously wrong in this country when it comes to election integrity. The censorship and violation of free speech is not limited to election integrity, for the same blatant censorship has happened extensively with regard to Covid-19, masks, lockdowns, and vaccines.

Anyone promoting the idea that the earth is flat would be considered to be ignorant of science or absolutely crazy by the vast majority of people, yet most would be kindhearted in their response to people holding to such ideas, and certainly would not call for censorship of people exercising their right to free speech in articles, speeches, or books about the subject.

People that say to "follow the science" with respect to the origin of Covid-19, the efficacy of hydroxychloroquine and of ivermectin as therapeutics, the efficacy and hazards of mandating the use of masks, the cost benefit analysis of local or nationwide lockdowns, the efficacy and safety of vaccines, and the accuracy of the 2020 election results are completely unscientific in rejecting any hypotheses or competing theories out of hand. The censorship of such competing ideas should be a wake-up call to every American regardless of political affiliation.

Intimidation Tactics

The intimidation tactics of Democrats, leftists, Marxists and their globalist puppet-Masters should be very strong evidence that there was something very wrong about the 2020 election. Nefarious actors use "direct action" as code words for inciting protests and riots in the streets when needed to intimidate elected officials. The violence perpetrated in lawless cities like Seattle and Portland in the summer of 2020 was used to give weight to the threat of Democrats and their cronies mobilizing four million rioters to hit the streets if the election did not go their way. It is reported that Chief Justice John Roberts was yelling at fellow Supreme Court justices about riots when they were considering whether to take up the Texas challenge of the hotly contested states.

The fact that whistleblowers or witnesses that questioned specifics about the 2020 election were harassed or even fired is evidence. The fact that a U.S. postal worker in Michigan was grilled by the investigator general office about how he managed to connect to a particular talk show host instead of examining his claims of election fraud is evidence. Thousands of affidavits collected by Rudy Giuliani, Bernie Kerik, and others presenting evidence of election fraud, some of whom were harassed or intimidated, is evidence.

RED, BLUE AND GRAY

The map on the cover of this book shows the status of the election late on election night and into the next morning. Red states were won by Donald Trump, blue states were won by Joe Biden, and the six gray states were too close to call and hotly contested.

Arizona

In Volume Three of the Navarro Report, Peter Navarro presents a chart entitled "Figure Two" on page 4 of that report that tabulates 254,722 potentially illegal votes cast in the 2020 election in Arizona, which is approximately twenty-four times the recorded Biden victory margin of 10,457 votes. Navarro asserts that there were 19,997 absentee ballots cast from addresses other than where voters legally resided, a total of 22,903 absentee ballots cast that were returned on or before the postmark date, a total of 157 double voters in the state, and 5790 "ghost" voters, which are instances when someone requests and submits a ballot under the name of a voter who no longer lives at the registered address for that voter.

Navarro asserts that there were 150,000 mail-in ballots cast by voters registered after the registration deadline, a total of 2000 votes cast by voters with no address on file, a total of 36,473 votes cast by noncitizen voters, a total of 5726 votes cast by out-of-state voters who voted in Arizona, and 11,676 "over-votes," which indicates a greater than 100% turnout of registered voters.

The Arizona Senate voted 16-14 to authorize a full forensic audit of the Maricopa County 2020 election, which proceeded after much opposition and litigation. Unlike other recounts or "audits" conducted around the country after the 2020 election, the Maricopa County full forensic audit was designed to count every physical ballot cast in the election, to count the number of votes cast for each candidate for president in the election, to examine the paper used for each ballot, whether or not mail-in ballots were folded to indicate the ballots were actually mailed to or from actual voters, and whether votes were fraudulently cast by machine, or by voters using pens.

At the time of this writing, the canvassing phase of the Maricopa County full forensic audit intended to verify that voters listed at physical addresses actually lived at those addresses had not yet started. The Attorney General under the Biden Regime, Merrick

Garland, threatened criminal charges against canvassers in this phase of the audit. The Maricopa County Board of Supervisors was refusing to comply with subpoena requests for routers and passwords that would permit the full forensic audit of the voter and tabulation machines used in the election.

Approximately twenty other states reportedly toured the facility used for the Maricopa County full forensic audit, indicating strong interest by the states in the process used to conduct the audit. The hand count of all of the physical ballots in the Maricopa audit will reveal the actual total of ballots cast, and the number of votes for president for each candidate. A big discrepancy between these numbers and the numbers reported by the electronic tabulation system at the conclusion of the 2020 election process would be a huge problem, as the certification of the election results in Arizona were based upon the electronic tabulation totals.

If the total votes cast in Maricopa County turn out to be 1.9 million ballots instead of the approximately 2.1 million ballots reported by the electronic tabulation system, the "over-votes" number in the Navarro report for Arizona would become zero, but all of the other potentially illegal votes that Peter Navarro details in his chart would still stand. If the audit reveals that there were 100,000 absentee ballots that were allegedly received, but were never folded or are shown to be filled in by machine, those ballots would not diminish any of the numbers in Peter Navarro's list of potential illegal ballots.

The Maricopa County forensic auditors made some stunning revelations at the July 15, 2021 hearing before the Arizona Senate. One of the most significant revelations was that there were 74,243 mail-in ballots received and counted that had no evidence that they were mailed to voters in the first place.

The auditors also revealed the fact that there were approximately 37,000 queries in the election system on March 11, 2021, which totally erased the logs of such queries prior to that date. Such activity suggests an effort to destroy evidence and cover up nefarious activity, and should prompt additional investigation by the auditors and perhaps criminal investigation.

In their audit, the full forensic auditors discovered that the election system was hacked on the day of the election, that approximately 10,000 voters in the 2020 election were added to voter rolls after Election Day, and that there were thousands of 2020 election voters who were removed from voter rolls after Election Day. All of these revelations should require further inquiry.

Another huge discovery was an internal email stating that election workers were to provide pens for voters to mark their ballots prior to Election Day, but that election workers "needed" to provide Sharpies to voters on Election Day, confirming what has been referred to as "Sharpiegate."

Election workers were told to provide Sharpies to voters on Election Day because Republican voters were expected to turn out to vote on that day. Sharpies were normally prohibited from being used to mark ballots because they are more likely to bleed through and spoil the ballot. The ballots in Maricopa County were double-sided, and it was also discovered that thinner paper was used for printing some of the ballots, which would dramatically increase the number of spoiled ballots.

Georgia

In Volume Three of the Navarro Report, Peter Navarro presents a chart entitled "Figure Three" on page five of that report that tabulates 601,130 potentially illegal votes cast in the 2020 election in Georgia, which is approximately fifty-one times the recorded Biden victory of 11,779 votes. Navarro asserts that there were 305,701 absentee ballots cast that were requested before or after the statutory period of time that permitted voters to request absentee ballots.

Navarro reports that in Georgia there were 10,315 dead voters, 395 double voters, 2560 felons that voted, 15,700 "ghost" voters,

66,247 voters under the age of eighteen, 1043 voters with no addresses on file, 2423 voters that were not registered on voter rolls, 20,312 out-of-state voters who voted in Georgia, and 40,279 voters who voted in counties where they did not legally reside.

Navarro points out that there was an inexplicable surge of 136,155 votes for Joe Biden at 1:34 am on November 4, 2020. This number seems unrealistically high compared to 29,115 additional votes for president Trump at that same time. The fact that there were similar inexplicable surges in the middle of the night in Michigan and Wisconsin may indicate a coordinated effort by nefarious actors to record illegal votes.

Republican observers were sent home from the Fulton County Georgia counting center, as they were told that counting would not continue until the morning. A burst pipe was given as a reason for the shutdown of counting, yet there were no records of that being a legitimate reason. Several people were caught in surveillance video after that time pulling cases of ballots out from under tables in the tabulation center, with the video footage showing that tens of thousands of votes were tabulated in the middle of the night. Two of these people recorded were also recorded during normal operation of the counting center passing what looked like a thumb drive between them.

Georgia spent over $100 million to purchase Dominion Systems voting equipment for all of Georgia's 159 counties. The Georgia executive branch entered into a consent decree with Stacy Abrams or her affiliated groups that was rubberstamped by the Georgia judicial branch without the knowledge or action by the legislature. This usurpation of the Georgia legislature authority over elections is concerning, but it also turns out that the temporary personnel firm known as "Happy Faces" that was hired to supply election workers in Georgia is owned in part by Stacy Abrams.

It is reported that Georgia hired 285 deputy registrars for the 2020 election that had the ability to alter voter rolls. This raises numerous questions for anyone curious about the integrity of the Georgia election process. Were any of these deputy registrars provided by Happy Faces? Could they have added underage voters to the voter rolls or recorded a request for absentee ballots from voters outside of the deadline? While observing the coverage of the 2020 Election Farce, I remember a news report following a particular person working in a cubicle with a stack of ballots entering information into the computer. This kind of activity, even if there was a legitimate reason for it, raises the specter of unlimited opportunity for tampering with election results, and should be unacceptable to anyone seeking election integrity.

Part of the agreement between Georgia and Stacy Abrams was that a consultant would be hired to observe the election process in Fulton County. The report filed by the consultant consists of essentially a diary of problems and concerns noted by the consultant in chronological order before, during, and after the November 3, 2020 election. The report of more than twenty pages details many concerns about the election process in Fulton County, but it is the report of a single observer in one county that could not physically be in all places at all times, so the actual concerns and problems with the 2020 election in Georgia are probably exponentially worse than detailed by the consultant in his report.

Similar to Arizona, the efforts by Georgia legislators to initiate a full forensic audit of the Georgia 2020 election statewide or in specific counties has been resisted by election officials and officials in the Georgia executive branch. It is reported that there has been a coordinated effort to intimidate whistleblowers that have been willing to come forward to report on what appears to be massive election fraud in Georgia.

Michigan

In Volume Three of the Navarro Report, Peter Navarro presents a chart entitled "Figure Four" on page six of that report that tabulates 446,803 potentially illegal votes cast in the 2020 election in Michigan, which is approximately 2.9 times the recorded Biden victory margin of 154,818 votes. Navarro asserts that there were 27,825 absentee ballots requested under the name of registered voters without their consent, 482 dead voters, 35,109 voters with no address on file, 174,384 voters with no corresponding voter registration numbers, 13,248 out-of-state voters who voted in Michigan, and 195,755 voting machine irregularities.

There was a pattern in election jurisdictions in several states where Republican observers were intimidated, harassed or physically blocked from observing several aspects of the election process, which were all violations of state law and any measure of election integrity and transparency that should be followed. The Wayne County counting center went so far as to cover over the windows after forcing out Republican observers. That may have been the counting center that was reported to have padlocked the doors to make sure Republican observers were kept out of the room.

Dilbert creator Scott Adams accurately stated that in Michigan, the election was "not transparent by force." I would like to add that the election was not transparent by design, and that there was a coordinated effort across multiple states or election jurisdictions to compromise transparency in the 2020 election. This kind of activity should cause the results of any election jurisdiction that permits such activity to be tossed out and a new election conducted. Such activities are not only evidence of election fraud; they are evidence that our nation has become a banana republic.

Nevada

In Volume Three of the Navarro Report, Peter Navarro presents a chart entitled "Figure Five" on page seven of that report that tabulates 220,008 potentially illegal votes cast in the 2020 election in Nevada, which is more than six times the recorded Biden victory margin of 33,596 votes. Navarro asserts that there were

15,000 absentee ballots cast from addresses other than where voters legally resided, 1506 dead voters, 42,284 double voters, 8000 voters with no address on file, 4000 noncitizen voters, 19,218 out-of-state voters who voted in Nevada, and 130,000 votes cast with signature matching errors.

Navarro asserts that the signature matching problems were a result of Clark County Nevada using machines to verify signatures on ballots instead of following state law requiring people to verify signatures. Navarro correctly asserts that the use of the machines in violation of state law, the fact that lower quality images were used for verification, and the lower machine settings used by election officials rendered the machines unreliable, and the results invalid.

Clark County, and especially Las Vegas, has been known for a long time as an election jurisdiction that has embraced all manner of election fraud. In addition to the standard corruption found in Clark County election operations, there were reports of bribery and payoff of voters throughout Nevada, which is a blatant violation of election laws.

Pennsylvania

In Volume Three of the Navarro Report, Peter Navarro presents a chart entitled "Figure Six" on page eight of that report that tabulates 992,467 potentially illegal votes cast in the 2020 election in Pennsylvania, which is approximately twelve times the recorded Biden victory margin of 81,660 votes.

Navarro also asserts that there were 10,000 absentee ballots counted that arrived after Election Day, 14,328 absentee ballots cast from addresses other than where voters legally resided, 58,221 absentee ballots that were returned on or before postmark dates, 9005 absentee ballots counted without a postmark, 8021 dead voters, 742 double voters, 7426 out-of-state voters who voted in Pennsylvania, 202,377 over votes, 1573 votes by people over 100 years old, and 680,774 poll watcher and poll observer abuses.

The pattern of blocking partisan observers from the verification of mail-in ballots, the verification of absentee ballot signatures, and the observing of the counting of votes in counting centers is an egregious violation of election transparency and fairness, and puts the United States right into the category of a banana republic. These actions in several states indicate a coordinated effort by nefarious actors to commit election fraud in order to steal the presidency, the Senate and Congress from the American people. In legal filings after the election, attorneys observed that "without meaningful observation of the ballot counting process, it is impossible to verify the legality of absentee and mail-in ballots."

Philadelphia has long been known as a cesspool of voter fraud and election fraud, as well as intimidation and harassment of voters and election process observers. The 2020 election farce emboldened nefarious actors to go all-in on election fraud in Pennsylvania. The magnitude of over-votes in the state is evidence of this. What 200,000 over-votes means, is that there were 200,000 more votes counted in the state in the 2020 election than there were registered voters in the state.

Doug Mastriano and other Pennsylvania state legislators are working tirelessly to initiate a full forensic audit similar to that conducted in Maricopa County Arizona. Resistance to those efforts indicates that the perpetrators of the election fraud are fully aware of what the results would be of such an audit. Arizona only had 16,000 over votes, but 200,000 over votes in Pennsylvania indicates that the ballot boxes were stuffed, or the machines counted votes multiple times.

One brave whistleblower came forward and signed affidavits certifying that he drove a tractor trailer truck load of ballots from New York to Pennsylvania. He sat around one location and was told to go to another location without giving him the standard transfer documentation. He was later told to park and leave his trailer, which was not where he left it when he showed up for work the next morning. In the 2020 election there were many instances of witnesses and whistleblowers being intimidated for coming forward to report suspicious activities. Several of these witnesses were employed by the United States Postal Service, and were harassed by postal inspectors or union thugs.

Wisconsin

In Volume Three of the Navarro Report, Peter Navarro presents a chart entitled "Figure Seven" on page ten of that report that tabulates 553,872 potentially illegal votes cast in the 2020 election in Wisconsin, which is more than twenty-six times the recorded Biden victory margin of 20,682 votes. Navarro asserts that there were 170,140 absentee ballots cast without an application required by state law, 234 double voters, 17,271 ballots harvested illegally, 216,000 votes cast by voters abusing the relaxed ID requirements of the "indefinitely confined" statute, 6848 out-of-state voters who voted in Wisconsin, and the November 4, 2020 3:42 AM vote spike of 143,379 votes for Joe Biden compared to 25,163 votes cast for Donald Trump recorded at the same time.

Although Wisconsin has more strict election laws than a lot of states, there were blatant violations of Wisconsin election law in the 2020 election. Navarro points out that the 17,271 ballots that were illegally harvested were cast at 200 polling places through illegal "Democracy in the Park" events that were advertised by the Biden campaign. Covid-19 was used as an excuse to dramatically increase the number of "indefinitely confined" voters that were permitted to vote without being required to provide photo IDs. Evidence has been collected of many of those same voters demonstrating that they were not confined.

Other States

Evidence of massive election fraud in the 2020 Election Farce is not limited to the six "gray" states. There are many other election jurisdictions around the country that have been reported to have had problems with the integrity of their election results. Our election system is so broken that groups are forming up in every state to push for full forensic audits in each state, including conservative states where President Trump won by large margins.

WHAT DOES A FULL FORENSIC AUDIT LOOK LIKE?

A full forensic audit of any process and the results generated by that process is simply a common sense approach to examining all aspects of the process, including the integrity of the process itself and the reliability and accuracy of the results generated. A full forensic audit of the 2020 election or any subset of the election could be used to expose fraud, or to simply identify ways to improve the design of the process and the control systems involved in assuring accuracy and integrity in the results.

A full forensic audit is a truth-seeking, fact-finding mission that is thorough and comprehensive. From what I know of the Maricopa County audit, the auditors are taking a very serious and meticulous approach that, when completed, will be above reproach. When you start with the approximately 2.1 million votes tabulated by Dominion voting systems, the first question to examine is how that number compares to the number of physical ballots in the possession of the auditors. A discrepancy in those numbers could mean that the electronic tabulation of votes was wrong, or that chain of custody issues led to a loss of physical ballots. Either of these would present a huge problem which would invalidate results.

A full forensic audit would require an examination of all of the electronic hardware and software used in conducting the election. The fact that the Maricopa County Board of Supervisors has been completely uncooperative with the audit process is a serious red flag that is a strong indicator of wrongdoing. The fact that Maricopa County used an election system with proprietary software that pro-

60

hibits transparency is a serious problem that should result in the immediate termination of contracts with such vendors.

A full forensic audit would chase down any and all allegations of any problems with the process or results under audit. Everything is fair game, regardless of political considerations, or whether something is purported to be scientific or a conspiracy theory. Honest auditors do not care about the status or demographics of fact witnesses or those making allegations. They are simply factfinders.

Allegations of counterfeit absentee ballots would lead factfinders to examine absentee ballots to see if there are creases that show evidence that the ballot was mailed to or from the absentee voter. It would lead truth seekers to examine for identical markings that would indicate machine generated ballots as opposed to ballots marked by hand by real people.

In order to audit ballots for the actual count of votes cast for each office, auditors conducting a full forensic audit would have to devise a system that accurately hand counted and verified ballots. The Maricopa County auditors devised such a system to reliably count, double check and verify the actual vote tallies for president and for the U.S. Senate race. The time that it takes to conduct such a hand count of all of the ballots is a weakness in the current system that places undue reliance on electronic tabulation, which would prompt auditors to consider alternative systems that they could recommend for future use.

If the Maricopa County full forensic audit revealed that there were 1.9 million paper ballots, and not approximately 2.1 million reported by the tabulation system, that alone would invalidate the certified election results. If the ballot count was within a few hundred votes, but the tally of the votes for the presidential race or the Senate race were dramatically different from the machine tabulation, the hand count of paper ballots would prevail. In that case, however, all of the ballot images captured by the electronic tabulation system, if those ballot images exist, would be examined.

The fact that the Maricopa County auditors revealed at a July 15, 2021 hearing that 74,243 absentee ballots were returned with no evidence that the ballots were originally sent to voters is a huge problem that would require further examination. Such revelations in an audit lead to more questions and the peeling back of more layers in order to get to the bottom of what happened.

During his interview on Steve Bannon's War Room with Peter Navarro on July 17, 2021, Arizona State Senator Sonny Borrelli said something about twenty-five voters being registered at a vacant house. Whether or not Borrelli was speaking hypothetically or was revealing or repeating a fact that the auditors found such a house, a full forensic audit should include a "re-canvassing" that examines the legitimacy of voter rolls in whole or in part.

A full forensic audit should examine the list of registered voters as of Election Day for aberrations, such as twenty-five people registered at a single-family home regardless of whether it was vacant or not. The list of registered voters eligible to vote in the election should also be compared to the list of actual voters to make sure that nobody voted that was not on the list of eligible voters as of Election Day. A forensic audit that finds that a jurisdiction cannot provide either of these lists would flag that as a problem. Auditors would examine the process by which voters are added or deleted from voter rolls.

A full forensic audit should examine any election jurisdiction that experienced uncertain or shifting numbers of absentee ballots yet to be counted. Any election jurisdiction that always seems to have difficulty conducting elections and reporting results in a timely fashion would also be carefully examined in a full forensic audit. Any jurisdiction that experiences an over-vote scenario where more votes are tabulated than registered voters in the jurisdiction would be a huge red flag, and should be carefully examined.

A full forensic audit would identify weaknesses and vulnerabilities in the election process, or in the manner by which the election was administered. Something as egregious as banning Republican observers from counting rooms, or from observing signature matching and the opening of ballots received by mail should lead auditors to immediately declare an election invalid. Blatant violations of chain of custody protocols should also invalidate election results.

Auditors conducting a full forensic audit of the entire 2020 election would flag the fact that there are states that do not have paper ballots as a serious breach of election integrity. We the People need not see the results of a full forensic audit nationwide in order to identify the thousands of breaches in election integrity. It just takes the tenacity of a handful of people that, like a dog, just won't let go of the bone.

There is a stark contrast between the full forensic audit being conducted in Maricopa County and the fake audit that Georgia conducted on November 14-15, 2020. Garland Favarito is a citizen of Georgia who initiated a lawsuit to examine the 2020 election in Fulton County Georgia. During a July 17, 2021 interview with Peter Navarro, Favorito revealed that the Georgia November "audit" had a 60% error rate in the tally sheets, that seven of the tally sheets were falsified, showing a total of 850 votes for Joe Biden and zero for President Trump, and that there were thousands of duplicate ballots.

Based upon the ballot images that were made public, Favorito said he would be amending his complaint to take additional steps to get to the truth. This illustrates the painstaking steps that must be taken in order to flesh out the facts related to the 2020 Election Farce. Sometimes ordinary citizens have to work very hard to get to the truth, especially when there are nefarious actors covering their tracks, hiding the evidence, obfuscating, and fighting you in court.

The full forensic audit of Maricopa County conducted by the auditors hired by the Arizona Senate may be the gold standard by which other states could conduct such audits of the 2020 election, or for future elections using the current broken election system, but such audits cannot be conducted in a timely fashion for states to certify the results of a federal election. The nefarious actors who conspired to commit massive fraud in the 2020 election knew that it would be impossible to conduct a full forensic audit in time to prove the fraud before electors had to be certified five weeks after the election. They were counting on it!

By contrast, the full forensic audit of any congressional district in a federal election in states that adopt the simple elements of this plan to restore election integrity could be quickly and accurately conducted between Federal Election Day and the date by which states are constitutionally required to certify electors. Without the use of electronic voting or the electronic tabulation of votes, and a fully transparent process, an audit would be simple.

If not for a vote of 16-14 in the Arizona Senate, the Maricopa County full forensic audit would not have been authorized. Let that sink in, dear patriot! The thorough, comprehensive fact-finding mission of the Arizona auditors would not have taken place if not for the vote of one Senator in Arizona. We the People must stand against all the forces of evil that are being arrayed against us in our fight for election integrity.

There is an abundance of evidence of election fraud that needs further investigation, and this should be obvious to anyone that has the slightest bit of intellectual curiosity about what actually happened during the 2020 election cycle. It is my informed belief that Joseph R Biden was selected as president, not elected. The Biden Regime is illegitimate, and is the greatest internal destructive force our nation has ever faced.

FOUR

Clear and Present Danger

THE UNITED STATES IS IN THE MIDST OF A COUP, A MARXIST TAKEOVER

I believe there are more instances of the abridgment of the freedom of the people by gradual and silent encroachments of those in power than by violent and sudden usurpations.

– James Madison

We all have the liberty to believe what we choose to believe, to hold opinions that we believe to be informed opinions, no matter what other people think about our beliefs or about us. We have the freedom to sincerely believe something, even though we may be wrong. It is one of the blessings of being an American.

What I express in this book are my opinions about the distress that I believe our nation is in, the great peril we face if we don't do something dramatic to change course, and proposals of the best ideas that I have been able to come up with to solve the problems in Gordian-knot cutting fashion.

ENEMIES, FOREIGN AND DOMESTIC

Members of the military and elected officials take an oath to defend the Constitution against all enemies, foreign and domestic. Millions of patriots believe as I do, that our nation and our Constitution are under constant and intense attack by foreign and domestic enemies of our Constitution. We can plainly see elected officials blatantly and defiantly undermining and attacking the Constitution of the United States. We the People must organize our peaceful efforts to defend our Constitution and our Republic from such attacks.

THE PARTY OF DIVISION, DESTRUCTION AND DEATH

The Democrat party will either self-destruct or destroy our constitutional Republic. Democrats are "all in" in their desperate attempt to fundamentally transform our nation. They are in a fight to the death. Democrats have overplayed their hand, and they are determined to take our Republic past the point of no return before We the People have a chance to get organized and get on the same page to stop them.

The Democrat party is the party of division. Democrats thrive on racial division. In fact, if Americans started living like we are in the post-racial country that the United States has become, race would be a nonissue to a colorblind society and the Democrat party would lose its raison d'être and cease to exist. Democrats don't truly want Blacks to prosper, because when Blacks prosper they leave the Democrat plantation.

The response to Covid-19 has given Democrats a new way to divide Americans, pitting us against each other: the masked against the unmasked, the vaccinated against the unvaccinated. It is reprehensible, but the (D) after a candidate's name running for office also stands for division.

The Democrat party is the party of destruction. Democrats destroy anything that is under their control for long enough for them to implement their destructive policies. Look at what they have done to cities under their control, and to the black communities that they lord over. Democrat policies have destroyed the nuclear family and traditional marriage. Democrats don't know how to build; they just know how to tear down. Many Democrats are waking up to that fact, especially among black and Latino communities. The (D) after a candidate's name stands for destruction.

The Democrat party is the party of death, and there is no greater evidence of that fact than the insane commitment to the murder of millions of innocent, unborn people. The national sin of abortion is the defining policy of the Democrat party. They have become so committed to perpetuating the barbaric practice that they have even embraced infanticide.

Democrat immigration policy promoting open borders actually creates a magnet for people to illegally cross into the United States, with thousands dying in the attempt to enter the country. Cartels are empowered to exploit thousands, with many being left behind to die. The same cartels take advantage of the open borders and bring deadly drugs into the United States, and the human trafficking that cartels are engaged in adds to the misery and death. This would stop if Democrats would support the securing of our borders. The (D) after a candidate's name stands for death.

Democrats know that half of Democrats will eventually wake up and realize that their leaders have exploited them to take our country in a direction that they do not agree with. Democrats know that they are short on time to accomplish their objectives, so they are brazen and outlandish in their methods and actions.

Whether the Democrat party self-destructs or destroys our Republic depends upon how many Democrats awaken to the fact that the Democrat party is the party of division, destruction, and death and flee the Democrat party. We the People can help them do so by asking them to unite with us to expose the 2020 Election Farce, and to help us restore integrity to federal elections.

TYRANNY RISING

We the People are witnessing tyranny rising, and will encounter resistance from liberals, globalists, and radical environmentalists as we seek to not only repudiate the rising tyranny, but to establish greater personal and economic liberty. Despite the yearning for liberty in the hearts of men, darkness descends upon the hearts of those in power, and we are seeing tyranny rising throughout most institutions in nations across the globe. Thankfully, people are awakening to the evil forces working to destroy our nation.

Covid-19

There is no doubt that Covid-19 is a dangerous and deadly disease, but there is much reason to believe that the disease was used as a basis to justify coordinated action by globalists to test the willingness of global populations to submit to draconian measures that were rolled out in response to the disease. As the truth comes out, I believe that we will find that the disease did not warrant the lockdowns, mask mandates, and the rush to give emergency approval to experimental vaccines. We will find that the truth was suppressed in order to implement a planned strategy for the subjugation of people under the iron boot of tyrants.

Thousands of tyrants around the world were eager to declare states of emergency and lock down economies, picking winners and losers as companies and workers were categorized as essential or nonessential. Great economic harm was done in order to test the compliance of citizens of most countries in order to prepare for what globalists openly call "The Great Reset."

Free speech was suppressed, for lockstep liars would not permit us to question any aspect of their tyrannical approach. While telling us to "follow the science," they denied us the opportunity of the very fundamental scientific approach of questioning hypotheses and seeking out the facts and evidence that support or refute each hypothesis or competing idea.

Questioning the number of deaths attributed to Covid-19 was forbidden. Promoting the efficacy of therapeutics such as hydroxychloroquine, azithromycin, zinc, and ivermectin would bring ridicule and censorship from social media titans. Plandemic, a documentary or movie promoting the idea that the Covid-19 pandemic was planned was banned by big tech.

United States citizens failed the test miserably, as we have witnessed millions of sheeple blindly accept what they have been fed, and not only comply with the draconian measures, but turn on fellow Americans that dared question the truth of what we were being told. The danger of Covid-19 is nothing compared to the dangers of the weaknesses exposed by the response of the American people under the heavy hand of thousands of little tyrants.

Tyranny of Technology

The rapid advancement of technology has the potential to bring greater liberty to all of humanity, but it also has the potential to enslave all of humanity. The concentration of the power of technology into the hands of a few is a threat to our liberty. Many of my libertarian friends that believe that we should not fear the establishment of monopolies seem to also believe that man is inherently good. History has shown that man too often yields to his sin nature, seeking to oppress his fellow man through the monopolization of various levers of control, including technology.

A government of the people, by the people and for the people will not use its power and authority to exploit and oppress its own citizens. Those governing by the consent of the governed would not dare lie to and betray the trust of the citizens that they serve. The federal government has so exceeded the limitations imposed by our founders that they cannot be trusted to refrain from using new technology to increasingly conduct warrantless surveillance on its citizens in order to protect its growing power and authority.

In this digital world that we live in, we are being used to conduct surveillance on ourselves. By accepting and using technology such as Google, Verizon and Facebook, and doing so under their terms of use and privacy policies, we have effectively granted the power to conduct surveillance on us without having a viable free-market alternative. Until such time as the federal government passes useful regulation to limit the encroachments on our privacy by these big tech companies, We the People run the risk of completely losing our privacy. Indeed, some involved in big tech companies have effectively told us that we no longer have a right to privacy, and that we should just get used to it.

It is curious to me that our federal government has established the Department of Homeland Security, consolidated and coordinated the sharing of information among various federal agencies and through the Patriot Act, has encroached upon our liberties, especially our right to privacy, but they have done nothing to secure our borders to staunch the flow of illegal immigrants that are pouring into our country, or to withdraw from the United Nations refugee resettlement program. Perhaps our government is less interested in national security than it is in controlling every aspect of our lives.

The federal government has been more than willing to permit big tech "winner take all" monopolies to be created because, by doing so, the federal government would eventually have access to an unprecedented volume of private information on all Americans. Never before in the history of mankind has it been possible for governments to be empowered with such levers of control over citizens. Our government is not only permissive in this, but is complicit in the use of technology to acquire incredible power over American citizens. Big government is merging with big tech.

In addition to threats to our privacy, rapidly developing technology that empowers companies like Google, Facebook, YouTube and Twitter to amass huge market shares of billions of people in their market segments has empowered them to individually and collectively control the information that we consume on a daily basis, which gives them the power to censor conservatives and to shape public opinion. Unprecedented censorship of conservatives by these and other big tech companies has already begun.

Many that are willing to accept the bread and circuses that the globalist elites want to use to control the masses are also more than willing to be spoon-fed by the liberal propaganda these companies espouse, but We the People must compel our government to use good old-fashioned trust-busting to break up these cartels before it's too late. Big tech has embraced liberalism, globalism and radical environmentalism, posing a threat to all of our liberties.

Climate Change

Now that tyrants have seen what they can get away with on a global scale with Covid-19 as a basis for their tyrannical actions, they will be emboldened to follow the same pattern using climate change as the global emergency that will give them justification for even more draconian measures taken against a compliant people.

THE DEEP STATE

People that deny the existence of what is known as "The Deep State" fail to acknowledge that there are people within our government that undermine United States interests, seeking to destroy our constitutional Republic, or merely misguided in their thinking that they are doing our country a service by working to sabotage a duly elected president of the United States.

I am sure that there are many nefarious actors in the bloated bureaucratic, administrative state that effectively work to neutralize the actions of duly elected leaders, but I have seen enough evidence to cause me to lose all trust in the Department of Justice, the FBI, the CIA, the NSA, and the United States Postal Service.

Rather than pursue the crimes of Hillary Clinton, the FBI gave her a pass on her illegal email servers. The FBI created a fake Russian dossier to try to damage president Trump, fabricating evidence in the process. The FBI had the Hunter Biden laptop in December 2019, yet did nothing with it, which impacted the Democrat primary. Bernie Sanders would have probably beat Joe Biden if the contents of the Hunter Biden laptop were properly dealt with by the FBI. The FBI is a corrupt anti-American organization.

The CIA has been known to meddle with elections in other countries, using what is called "Hammer and Scorecard" as they implement a "Color Revolution," according to Darren Beatty of Revolver News. It is quite possible that these tools were used in the 2020 election to give Joe Biden the win, as well as to deliver the Senate and Congress to the Democrats, perhaps with the involvement of CIA operatives. It would be nice to know the whole truth about what was going on in Benghazi during the September 11, 2012 attack on the consulate, as well as the toppling of Mubarak in Egypt and Qaddafi in Libya, as well as the rise of ISIS.

We can't trust the Department of Justice, for they sat back and did nothing during the greatest election fraud ever perpetrated, claiming there was nothing wrong with the election, when it was obvious to anyone with a little bit of curiosity and common sense that the 2020 election was a farce. The Department of Justice under Bill Barr also allowed the most valuable federal witness in United States history, Jeffrey Epstein, to die while in custody.

Instead of recognizing the value of Epstein as a witness and taking extraordinary measures to protect him from harming himself or from being harmed by others, the Department of Justice under Bill Barr did nothing, perhaps to protect the many witnesses that Epstein could have testified against by facilitating his death. The script could have been written by anyone: video recorders that did not function, guards that changed their testimony, a failed attempt at "suicide" that did not prompt extreme measures to protect the most valuable federal witness in United States history.

How is it that Jeffrey Epstein was the most valuable federal witness in United States history? Epstein had incriminating evidence on dozens, if not hundreds, of people in positions of power. Shortly after the death of Epstein, the FBI descended upon his private island to confiscate all of the evidence. One can only imagine the kind of evidence that Epstein had on numerous people listed on his airplane roster, including former president Bill Clinton. With the death of Jeffrey Epstein we will never know how some in our government are corrupt or compromised.

The 2020 election proved that we can no longer trust the United States Postal Service to handle any aspect of our elections. The truth will hopefully be known someday, but there are many allegations that have been made in sworn affidavits about nefarious actions committed by USPS personnel. Postal Service workers are unionized, and it should be assumed that they are predominantly left-leaning, but certainly union leadership is dominated by partisan union thugs that would eagerly participate in stealing elections.

As the truth becomes known about the events of January 6, 2021, I am confident that deep state actors will be implicated in what really happened on that day. I acknowledge that President Trump made some bad decisions along the way, but many of his supporters have been falsely accused of wrongdoing on that day. We the People have seen too much to accept the false narratives of the left and their deep state operatives.

CHINA PLAN FOR GLOBAL DOMINATION

China is the greatest threat to liberty in human history. They are close to realizing their 100 year plan for global domination. Using the pretext of the benefits of "free trade," the entrenched establishment political class and United States business interests have sold out the security and sovereignty of the United States to the Chinese Communist Party.

While United States business has been hamstrung by environmental policies, China has enjoyed increasing trade and manufacturing dominance because they have had no environmental constraints placed upon them, and they have a centralized, command economy with 1.4 billion slaves that they deploy in their quest for global domination.

China has been waging economic warfare against the United States for decades. While skillfully avoiding a kinetic conflict, they have been gaining strength in every area, preparing to surpass the United States in every measurable way, including the ability to wage kinetic warfare.

Fifty years ago, "made in China" was synonymous with low-quality manufactured goods. The present-day banner that I imagine over the map of China is "Made by the USA." The United States is almost single-handedly responsible for the rise of China. In the not-too-distant future, I fear that the banner over the United States will read "Owned by China." China is determined to own the United States and its resources, and to subject the population of United States citizens as indentured servants of China. The United States is on its way to becoming a tributary state to the great Dragon unless We the People compel our nation to take immediate and decisive retaliatory action against China. Our beef is not with the Chinese people, it is with the Chinese Communist Party.

THE BIDEN REGIME

Joe Biden was not elected president on November 3, 2020; he was SELECTED president by the perpetrators of the greatest election fraud in history. This will become clear as the truth that is still available for us to discover is exposed. Much of the truth has been covered up and distorted or blended in with the fraud so that it cannot be discovered, but I believe that Democrats also stole at least four Senate seats and a couple of dozen congressional seats.

In my opinion, the 2020 Election Farce has empowered the Biden Regime, which is also a farce. I acknowledge that Joe Biden occupies the power seat, but he is simply a puppet president of others that are pulling the strings in the background. This is obvious to everyone, including our allies and adversaries, who must be laughing at the banana republic that the United States has become.

Our nation is in greater distress than we have ever seen. We face multiple crises at home and abroad, but our nation no longer has the national character that it had at our founding, or during the Civil War, the Great Depression, and World War II. We are weak internally and we face unprecedented external forces, primarily from China, but also from Iran, North Korea and the globalists that want to establish a New World Order. Technology has advanced to the point where it could enslave us overnight. An EMP attack or cyber-attack could cripple our nation. And we face all of these perils with the illegitimate Biden Regime in power, as they do everything they can to destroy our constitutional Republic.

Open Borders, Refugees and Radical Islamic Jihad

Even before being sworn-in in a farce of an inauguration, Joe Biden was advertising that our southern border was open for the infiltration of illegal persons and goods. Joe Biden, under the direction of his puppet-masters, and empowered by his minions, has violated Article 4 Section 4 of the Constitution, whereby the federal government is charged with defending the states against invasion. They have invited an invasion that has empowered and enriched Mexican drug cartels, which undermines the Mexican government. The Biden Regime has dramatically increased the number of United Nations refugees, and they have embraced the radical Islamist nation of Iran. All of these actions are treasonous acts that undermine United States security and sovereignty.

Energy Dependence

After his sham inauguration, Joe Biden proceeded to sign numerous executive orders. He probably did not have the mental capacity to clearly state the purpose of very many of those executive orders, yet sign them he did. One of the most deleterious executive orders was canceling the Keystone pipeline, which will create greater dependence upon foreign oil by the United States. Democrats don't want the United States to be energy independent. Later, Joe Biden canceled oil leases, particularly in the Alaska national wildlife refuge, or ANWR. With the stroke of a pen, and directed by unseen powers, Joe Biden wiped out thousands of American jobs.

Institutionalized Election Fraud

The Biden Regime wasted no time in the introduction of HR-1, which would institutionalize election fraud. Using the power that they secured by massive election fraud, Democrats are shamelessly and brazenly attempting to eliminate every opportunity that We the People have to restore election integrity. Democrats know that their time is limited before the truth comes out and before they lose their majority in Congress. They don't care, they are drunk with power. Just like when they passed Obamacare knowing that they would likely lose the house, Democrats are doubling down on destructive measures and are willing to do anything to get them passed.

Critical Race Theory

The Democrat party is the party of division, and they are using every means they can to divide Americans based upon race. They are trying to cram Critical Race Theory down the throats of Americans before we even have a chance to catch our breath. Democrats don't realize that they have overplayed their hand, We the People know that they have overplayed their hand, and that there is a movement among our black brothers and sisters and our Latino brothers and sisters that is putting America first and rejecting the lies of the Democrat party.

Part of the Democrat calculus in throwing everything at us at the same time is that We the People will be so distracted and disorganized that they will succeed in many of their initiatives. Critical Race Theory is one initiative that we must stop.

Destruction of the Military

The Biden Regime is working at breakneck speed to double down on the progress that the Barack Obama administration made in undermining, transforming and destroying the United States military. They are trying to purge the military of all patriots. They are trying to indoctrinate our service members with the heinous notion that the very Constitution that they are sworn to defend, against all enemies foreign and domestic, is the source of systemic racism in this country. The only systemic racism in this country comes from the Democrat party.

The military is the most trusted institution in the country, and the most diverse institution in the country. If Democrats succeed in destroying the United States military, they will destroy our nation. Democrats have likewise sought to destroy all law enforcement agencies, from local police departments to ICE and Customs and Border Control. They have succeeded in destroying the credibility and trust in the FBI and CIA, and are trying to do the same thing with law enforcement and the military.

Targeting Dissidents

In addition to targeting patriots in the military, the Biden Regime is seeking to classify America-first, liberty minded patriots as white supremacists and domestic terrorists. There were some bad actors on January 6, 2021 in what they falsely described as an insurrection, but they have gathered up ordinary Americans that were led to believe that they were permitted to be in the Capitol building, and they have rounded up many that didn't even enter the Capitol building. The estimated 14,000 hours of video recordings would likely show that the January 6, 2021 "insurrection" was really a deep state operation to entrap peaceful, patriotic U.S. citizens.

The Biden Regime is holding some of these innocent people in solitary confinement while permitting thousands of arsonists, looters, and rioters to go free without charging them with any crime or requiring bail. Even some Democrat lawmakers raised money to bail out "peaceful protesters" in Portland, Oregon and Seattle, Washington. This too, is a farce.

Democrats, the Deep State, and the Biden Regime are targeting patriotic, Trump supporting, America-first patriots in their efforts to classify them as "domestic terrorists." They are specifically going after groups like Proud Boys, Oath-Keepers, and Three Percenters. These groups, and most of the patriots targeted for harassment are not racists, but rather patriotic Americans concerned about the distress that our nation is in.

Infrastructure Farce

The infrastructure bill that Democrats are seeking to pass through Congress looks nothing like spending on infrastructure, but rather an example of political payoffs, buying votes, and of implementing the Cloward and Piven strategy to break the bank of the U.S. Treasury in order to destroy our country. After all, the Democrat party is the party of destruction.

An example of infrastructure spending that would be very worthy of consideration would be a plan to irrigate dry Western states by creating reservoirs to hold water, dams to generate energy, and pipelines to transport water from where it is abundant to where it is desperately needed. Such a project would provide abundant water to Western states, it would create large reservoirs of water in case of drought, which we know the Bible has predicted will come, and would generate clean energy. It would also alleviate flooding in states that have too much water at times.

Democrats don't want solutions to problems because they simply want to preserve their power at all costs. They simply will not accept anything that would shed a positive light on a president like Donald J Trump, the Republican Party, or patriotic Americans. They are the party of division, destruction and death, and their primary tool is deception. So their infrastructure bill is a total farce, masking their true nature and intent.

Middle-East

Democrats never gave President Donald Trump credit for the Abraham Accords, whereby several Arab states made peace with Israel in 2020. Upon assuming power, the Biden Regime wasted no time in setting the Middle-East region on fire. They empowered Iran, Hezbollah, and Hamas and undermined the safety and security of Israel. Israel endured the onslaught of about 4500 rockets fired into Israel from Gaza and exercised great restraint, yet endured criticism from the Biden Regime and the United Nations.

The Biden Regime is the laughingstock of the international community. Joe Biden was mocked and ridiculed at the G7 summit and Vladimir Putin made him look like the senile old man that he is. The only thing that must be encouraging our allies and keeping our adversaries in check is that they know what the truth is about the 2020 election, and they know that We the People will fix the problem in due time.

Our nation has been in distress for a long time, but with the theft of the 2020 election in the context of all of the other global developments, we are in greater distress than ever. The presidency, the House of Representatives and the Senate were all stolen from United States citizens, and as a result, our nation has been stolen. We are in the midst of a Marxist coup, and the very survival of our constitutional Republic is at stake.

THE GREAT RESET

Talk of a New World Order instituted by global elites, the collapse or reset of the global financial system, and such was dismissed as conspiracy theory for the longest time, but Klaus Schwab, executive chairman of the World Economic Forum, recently using the term "The Great Reset" has brought the talk of conspiracy theory to an end. They are very open with their plan, and it is not good for the middle class in the United States, or for liberty.

A strong middle class in the United States has been the greatest deterrent to such a reset of the global financial system, but with recent events and the doubling down by the Biden Regime to wreak economic havoc, we are on the cusp of such an event. The stage is set for globalists to use the impending collapse of the global financial system as an excuse to introduce their plan to rescue the global markets and to usher in the New World Order that they have been dreaming of for decades.

Governments and central banks have recognized that it will be impossible for governments to bail out banks and other sectors of the economy when the next collapse comes. Preparations have been made by the International Monetary Fund for Special Drawing Rights to be granted to countries based upon the size of their economies. They are ready to introduce a new, global currency to usher in a new global economy. We hear talk of negative interest rates, a cashless financial system, and bail-ins, where banks are bailed out by appropriating depositor funds.

There is an unholy alliance of big government statists, big banks, big business, big insurance, big tech, big media, big energy, big pharma and any other sector that has been consolidated for the purpose of establishing a New World Order under a single global government. American businesses that have become multinational conglomerates are no longer loyal to the United States. In the old days it used to be said that what was good for General Motors was good for America, what was good for United States business was good for America. That is no longer true. What is good for small businesses in America is good for America, but what is good for big business is no longer necessarily good for America.

Brexit and other nationalist movements among European Union nations that are seeking independence from the EU, as well as the anti-globalist, anti-establishment liberty movement that is afoot in the United States and other nations is an existential threat to the globalist New World Order agenda. These movements could prompt the early implementation of the globalist plan of triggering a collapse of the global financial system. Europe is in the process of committing suicide, so the United States is the greatest obstacle to the globalist agenda to form a New World Order.

FIVE

A Call to Action

WAKE-UP CALL TO PATRIOTS AND CHRISTIANS FOR ACTION AND REVIVAL

If my people, which are called by my name, shall humble themselves, and pray, and seek my face, and turn from their wicked ways; then will I hear from heaven, and will forgive their sin, and will heal their land.

    – 2 Chronicles 7:14

The message from God in 2 Chronicles 7:14 was intended for His people, Israel, but Christians in America today are at liberty to claim by faith and believe that if we Christians, called by the name of Christ, shall humble ourselves, and pray, and seek the face of God, and turn from our wicked ways; that God will hear from heaven, will forgive our sin, and will heal our land.

The Bible teaches us that, to whom much is given, much shall be required. Those of us that profess to be Christians bear a higher level of accountability to God for our stewardship of the liberty and the blessings that he has bestowed upon us. If there was ever a time for American Christians to repent in sackcloth and ashes, now is that time.

Our country needs revival. Our churches need revival. We as individual Christians need revival. The Bible says that in the end times, before Jesus can return, there will first be a falling away. It is quite likely that we are seeing that falling away, but just as there are many examples in Scripture of God sparing or postponing his judgment of Israel, we may see God spare his judgment on the United States a little while longer if we seek revival.

81

Pastors need to show some leadership and start preaching against the evils of liberalism and big government. Start speaking the truth and forget about the muzzle that has been placed upon you by a tyrannical government. Congregations and their pastors have failed to speak the truth because of the threat of the loss of tax deductibility of contributions. Folks, is there not a cause? Should we have permitted this great evil for the last fifty years? Does not the church in general and pastors in particular bear much responsibility for the current state of our country? We the People are responsible and we must accept that responsibility. We the People that are Christians bear an even greater share of responsibility.

The Albert Plan calls for a flat tax with no deductions or exemptions that will completely eliminate charitable deductions, but it also calls for the elimination of property taxes. These changes may offset each other, but even without these potential changes, we should have been doing the right thing all along. We the People that are Christians have shamefully allowed government to place a muzzle upon us, and have allowed political correctness to stop us from speaking the truth, as we are commanded to do by Scripture.

Many Christians have refrained from political activity because they have considered it to be a dirty, tainted business. Our founding fathers were deeply involved in political discourse and action, and did so predominantly as believers. They did not advocate for the separation of church and state, but rather demonstrated that their mandate that government not establish a religion was rooted in the reality that religion absolutely permeated everything that our founders did. The prohibition was against the establishment of a religion by government, not a prohibition of religious conviction of citizens having an impact upon the government.

We must get back to the founding principles of a God fearing people that are intimately involved in political discourse and action. Our nation needs the leadership of Christian men and women that have the backbone to stand up and fight for that which is right.

Christians must reject the passive approach that Christians have taken in the past that has accelerated the downward spiral of our nation and become active in advocating for truth and righteousness in the political process. Is there not a cause? Are we to sit back and do nothing, allowing evil to prevail in the world because we are eagerly awaiting the return of the Lord? We as Christians must recognize that simply voting in elections is not enough. As in the days of the founders of this nation, we must actively promote liberty and resist tyranny.

May we as Christians in this country restore our nation to the Judeo-Christian values that our nation was founded upon so that our nation may once again be blessed by God as no other nation has. I believe that we are in the last days, and are witnessing the falling away that was prophesied, but God's strength is made perfect in weakness, so let us not allow our weakness to hold us back from taking our country back.

ORGANIZE FREEDOM CELLS

We the People must form groups of like-minded patriotic Americans through which we may have our collective voices heard and our actions coordinated for maximum impact, so that we can take immediate action to take our country back. We must establish or join what I call "Freedom Cells" in order to do this. It is time that we conservatives try a little community organization, because Democrats don't have a monopoly on community organization!

Establish or join several Freedom Cells of any configuration that makes sense to you. We all belong to various groups, and we should each consider organizing those affinity groups for such a cause as this. Some patriots may form Freedom Cells of immediate or extended family, church groups, friends, neighbors, veterans groups or any other affinity group imaginable. Perhaps the most important Freedom Cell that each and every one of us should join or establish is within our local election precinct.

Hold monthly meetings of Freedom Cells with other patriots to discuss ideas and to take coordinated action to solve the serious problems that our country faces. If you like the ideas that I present in this plan, promote the bold ideas of this plan, or a plan of similar magnitude and direction to like-minded patriots, encouraging them to form a Freedom Cell with you, or to form Freedom Cells among their other affinity groups. It is important to have a bold, comprehensive and transformational plan of action. Use *The Albert Plan* as a starting point and form Freedom Cells to identify problems, discuss potential solutions and identify specific action steps that can be coordinated to take our country back.

In short, it is what we make of it. Freedom Cells should be established and operate as a network of self-organizing, autonomous, independent units of freedom loving Americans. We the People in each Freedom Cell are the true source of the collective power of the whole, just as it should be with our government. We the People are the Minutemen, and we are served by those who volunteer as Founding Fathers, Sons of Liberty, and Patriots to help organize, educate and facilitate communication among our members.

Some Freedom Cell Minutemen will self-identify as Freedom Cell Patriots to provide leadership at the precinct level. Some will self-identify as Freedom Cell Sons of Liberty to provide leadership at the county and congressional district level, and some will self-identify as Freedom Cell Founding Fathers to provide leadership at the state and national level.

We need not apologize for the use of Founding Fathers, Sons of Liberty or Minutemen to name the different leadership levels, because strong conservative women are eager and competent to contribute their leadership skills at any level, and they will not be offended or hesitant to join groups with fathers, sons or men in the names. Let feminists have a meltdown in their safe spaces!

Those who join Freedom Cells as Founding Fathers, Sons of Liberty or Patriots are simply volunteering their time and talent to serve as leaders of the movement to promote and implement *The Albert Plan* to save our Republic. The only power that those that volunteer and self-identify in positions of leadership will have to influence or control anything will be earned by effective service to We the People, the Freedom Cell Minutemen.

The communication, organization and action of Freedom Cells as a whole should begin at the local level, bubble up and percolate through the network, and result in local action all over the country. We the People must organize a grassroots liberty movement, not a top-down hierarchy. We must guard against establishment types hijacking this movement like they did the Tea Party movement.

The traditional model of organizing for political activism has predominantly been one of people that call themselves leaders that want to be the top pyramid on top of the pyramid with as many followers and volunteers as they can organize supporting them. This model must be discarded for one where the pyramid is inverted and each patriot that self identifies as a leader is seeking to educate, organize, inspire, motivate, and serve as many like-minded patriots as they can. The leader in this servant-leader model is crouched down supporting the inverted pyramid like Charles Atlas, supporting the world on his shoulders.

Transformational Conservatism

The terms fiscal conservative, social conservative and national defense conservative are pretty thoroughly understood. We the People must engage in what I call Transformational Conservatism in order to save our Republic.

The goals of Transformational Conservatism are to restore the Constitution, restore the balance of power, repudiate the entrenched establishment political class, restore fiscal sanity, restore our national security, restore our national prosperity, restore our national sovereignty, and to humbly ask our Creator to forgive us of our national sins and restore His blessings upon our land.

Prudent Populism

Transformational conservatives recognize the need for a bold, comprehensive, and transformational plan to accomplish these goals. We recognize the need to organize and to take action to save our country, and do so for as long as it takes. Liberals will describe us as populists and our ideology as populism, which they will use as derogatory terms. We must describe our ideology as prudent populism similar to that which led to the birth of our nation.

We the People are simply pursuing the principles laid out by our founding fathers. We do not believe in mob rule, and will not tolerate being described as an angry mob. We believe, as our founding fathers did, that government derives its power from the consent of the governed. We believe in government of the people, by the people, and for the people.

Prudent populism is how we should describe the organization and activism of We the People that form Freedom Cells so that we may restore our constitutional Republic as our founders intended. We cannot take our country back without populism. We need a movement of patriots to get the job done. Let us not allow liberals to disparage our patriotism.

New American Nationalism

If we are to save our nation from destruction, we must embrace rational and prudent nationalism. We desperately need an era of New American Nationalism. Liberals will have disparaging things to say about any effort advocating for increased nationalism. To them, nationalism is a derogatory term that they equate with isolationism, protectionism and xenophobia. They are entitled to their opinions, but we must push back with the truth.

The truth is that lax border security and immigration policy has compromised our national security. We are not xenophobic if we press the pause button on all immigration so that we may have a national discussion about immigration and national security. We are not xenophobic if we stop the flow of refugees under the United Nations Refugee Resettlement Program in order to assess the risks. We have been sold a bill of goods by the United Nations and the establishment political class. We should not allow name-calling by liberals to dissuade us from doing what is right for our country, including the imposition of a moratorium on work-visa immigration programs that have been robbing Americans of jobs.

The truth is that we have exported our prosperity along with millions of jobs because the entrenched establishment political class struck an evil bargain with globalists and crony capitalists. It is prudent and rational for us to examine our international trade policy and take steps to put America first. We have allowed our generosity as a free people to be taken advantage of to our detriment, and to the detriment of the world. Instead of tying our hands behind our backs, we should insist on secure, strategic trade. We the People must repudiate globalism and put American interests first.

Trade between countries should be win-win. It is not a zero-sum game. Our trading partners can be better off without making the United States worse off. The United States needs to quickly return to being a net exporting country and repatriate millions of jobs. We will gladly help other nations improve their standards of living, but we do not have to impoverish the American middle class in order to do so.

America has been uniquely blessed by God, and we are the most generous nation the world has ever seen. When we defeat an enemy, we rebuild their nation and require nothing more than enough land to bury our dead. What nation in the history of the world has ever operated that way? We need not apologize for the strength or prosperity of our nation. We should accept and be grateful for the greatness of our nation and acknowledge from Whom our blessings flow. We should recognize that liberals do not share our values, and that there are many people around the world that despise America because of our prosperity and liberty.

We must pursue New American Nationalism by strengthening our military and returning to a policy of speaking softly and carrying a big stick. We must rebuild the trust and confidence of our allies and reestablish fear and respect from our adversaries. The United States must restore its reputation for doing the right thing. We must restore the national sovereignty of the United States.

Disproportionate Share of Influence

Political activism, by its very nature, is the pursuit of a disproportionate share of influence. Everyone engaged in the political process is trying to magnify their influence in order to accomplish an objective. There are those that seek a disproportionate share of influence for evil purposes, and there are those that seek a disproportionate share of influence for the common good. Ideologues on the left probably earnestly believe that they are seeking the common good, and ideologues on the right believe that they are seeking the common good. The common good, which includes personal and economic liberty, is in the eye of the beholder.

We the People that desire to save our Republic must work diligently to use our time, talent and treasure to secure a disproportionate share of influence so that we may restore the Constitution and set our country on the right path again. We must not be bashful about seeking a disproportionate share of influence, and we must not passively allow ideologues on the left or the entrenched establishment political class of both parties in the vast middle that seek power for their own self-aggrandizement to continue to hold their disproportionate share of influence.

The Liberty Movement

For many years there has been a growing movement among like-minded patriotic Americans who realize that our country has been on the wrong track. People recognize that our nation is in distress. They recognize there are many problems that need urgent attention. People ask more and more frequently, "What can we do?" This growing Liberty Movement manifested itself in the Tea Party Movement that quickly spread nationwide after the election of Barack Obama and the passage of Obamacare.

It seems that the Tea Party Movement was co-opted by self-serving opportunists, and did not fully harness the energy behind the movement of patriotic Americans. The Liberty Movement again manifested itself by strongly supporting the anti-establishment candidacies of Donald Trump and Ted Cruz during the 2016 Republican primary, where they combined for approximately two-thirds of primary votes.

The Liberty Movement coalesced behind Donald Trump and gave him a decisive victory over Hillary Clinton, which even seemed to surprise Donald Trump himself. Donald Trump did not start a movement, he was a manifestation of the Liberty Movement, and We the People must figure out how we can better organize and sustain the Liberty Movement without allowing the focus to be on one primary person.

Move as One, Speak as One

Liberal Democrats can be described as lockstep liars, calling good evil and evil good, just as the Bible told us would happen in the end times. It will be difficult to get liberty loving patriots to move as one and speak as one, but it can be done. It must be done if We the People are to save our Republic.

It is amazing to watch synchronized swimmers move in unison with the same choreographed routine. More amazing is to observe huge flocks of birds in flight that turn on a dime, moving in unison in response to some unseen power that moves them. There is no apparent leader of the flock that mesmerizes us with their acrobatic antics, but we know that it is instinct put there by God. Just as amazing to watch, is the great schools of fish doing exactly the same thing underwater with such grace.

We the People that form Freedom Cells in a self-organizing, self-directing way must figure out how we can move as one and speak as one with countless other like-minded patriots in order to implement the bold, comprehensive, and transformational changes that are enumerated in *The Albert Plan to Save America: 2020 Edition.*

Focus on a Person or a Plan?

The problem with the focus being on the person running for any particular office is that there isn't enough continuity among candidates from election to election, or among candidates running for various offices in the same election. If we advocate for the same plan in overwhelming numbers, the focus would then be on the plan, and not so much on the person running for each office. We the People need to show a little community organization by rallying under the banner of the bold, comprehensive, transformational plan we need to implement to save our Republic.

A Point on the Horizon

Organizing countless patriots around a bold, comprehensive, transformational plan is similar to fixing a point on the horizon that represents the full implementation of the plan. We keep pressing toward the mark, adjusting if we find ourselves off course a little bit. Or if we look at the analogy of rowing a boat, we keep rowing in the direction of the point on the horizon.

Expanding a little bit on the analogy of rowing a boat to the point on the horizon, Freedom Cell Minutemen are analogous to the people rowing in the boat, and the Freedom Cell Patriot is analogous to the helmsman that is steering the rudder and calling cadence to those rowing. Those rowing know the goal, the point on the horizon, but they have to trust the helmsman to steer in the right direction as they pull on the oars. Minutemen have limited time to contribute, and they will look to Patriots for guidance on how they can best use their limited time for the cause.

The Need for Warriors and Gladiators

Whether you agree or not with everything that Donald Trump says or does, you have to recognize and respect the fact that he is willing to fight the battles as they come up. We need warriors that will fight and not give up. We need gladiators that can fight many battles simultaneously and not faint. Leftist Democrats are locked in mortal combat. They are in a fight to the death, and most people in the silent majority have no clue that we are in that battle.

If We the People organize Freedom Cells in overwhelming numbers all over the country, we can train up and equip warriors and gladiators from within our ranks and support them when they present themselves as candidates for office. Our sheer numbers would diminish the influence of campaign cash.

The Chinese probably have a 100 year plan, whereas most Americans always seem to be focused on the next election, not twenty or fifty years into the future. We must recognize that we are engaged in a long-term war, and that we must therefore conduct warfare accordingly. We can't just go out and vote, and expect to win. We must be engaged in the fight day in and day out.

Liberty is Decentralized and Distributed

Block chain technology is a decentralized, distributed open ledger system that uses technology to securely record transaction data that is next to impossible to alter without leaving evidence of the alteration. It is this technology that has empowered people to create crypto-currencies like bitcoin. Like block chain technology, true liberty is likewise decentralized, distributed and transparent.

Not only is block chain technology a good picture of what true liberty should look like, but new technologies like block chain give us the ability to secure greater liberty. New technologies could also be used to concentrate power and bring greater tyranny if we are not diligent in assuring that they are used for good. Organizing for political activism should be decentralized and distributed.

Historically, political power has been centralized and concentrated in few hands, but with modern technology we can organize Freedom Cells to be autonomous, decentralized and distributed. Self-organizing and self-governing collections of patriots of any size and shape that the individuals within each Freedom Cell desire to have will shun entrenched establishment political class types that seek to concentrate power in a few hands.

There are many groups that exist today on the conservative side of the political spectrum that are not properly organized to function in a decentralized and distributed way. They may have the best of intentions, but if they operate in a centralized fashion they are more likely part of the problem, and not part of the solution. Associate with them and learn all you can from them, and have fellowship with them, but don't expect to accomplish much. Perhaps 90% of the people in these groups are potential Freedom Cell members, but there will be some that will not want to give up their quest for concentrating power.

Cellular Structure

Some of my squeamish friends that don't realize the nature of the warfare that we are engaged in are apprehensive about using Freedom Cells to describe the groups that I am seeking to organize. I find it entirely appropriate to use Freedom Cells to describe what I am trying to organize, and I am confident that there are 30 million patriots that will have no problem with the term.

Election precincts look like individual cells on a map. A map of New England towns looks the same way, as there isn't a square foot of property in New England that is not part of a town. A map of New England towns looks like a honeycomb, or cells to me. Zoom in and you'll see precincts in the same way. Greenville County South Carolina has approximately 150 voter precincts. There are a little over 3000 counties in the United States that also look like cells. Congressional districts look like cells, and states look like cells. The most basic Freedom Cell is the individual. We the People have the liberty to define Freedom Cells any way that we choose to.

A Campaign of One

The way that any one of us can function as a Freedom Cell, is to wage a "Campaign of One." As someone wisely once said, "no man is an island unto himself," so I am not suggesting that we all operate independently of each other. What I am suggesting is that while working collaboratively with other like-minded patriots in a variety of Freedom Cells that we form or join, we have the liberty and the duty to conduct our own "Campaign of One."

Although I self-identify as a Freedom Cell Founding Father, and I am pursuing a rather ambitious plan to organize 30 million like-minded patriots, I am also conducting my own "Campaign of One." As I try new things and learn new things, I will be sharing what I consider to be best demonstrated practices in the limited scope of activities that I can pursue with my limited time and resources. I certainly hope to leverage my time, talent, and treasure for greater impact by recruiting, training, mentoring and inspiring others to follow the trails that I might blaze and accomplish things for the Liberty Movement that I have not yet imagined.

I encourage you, dear patriot, and other like-minded patriots, to not sit around and wait for somebody to tell you what to do, but rather to rise up and begin your "Campaign of One." If you are unsure of what to do, simply ask another Freedom Cell member what you can do to help.

Planting a Bamboo Forest

After decades of recognizing that our nation is in distress, watching that distress intensify, and experiencing the frustration of recognizing the problems our nation faces without seeing anybody stepping up to articulate what I thought to be the obvious solutions, I found myself in a position where I had the time and the unction to write *The Albert Plan to Save America*. Without realizing what I was doing, I embarked on my own "Campaign of One."

I have come to realize that over the last several years, I have been doing something that is similar to planting a bamboo forest. A bamboo forest does not grow overnight, in fact it takes three to five years after bamboo is planted for it to sprout, but when it does start to grow it grows very rapidly for about two months. My hope is that what I have been working on for the last few years will suddenly and rapidly grow in a fashion similar to a bamboo forest. I will do what I can, dear patriot, to leverage your efforts in the Liberty Movement, but I encourage you to not be discouraged if you find that your efforts don't bear immediate fruit.

Liberty Evangelism

Conducting or waging a "Campaign of One" involves becoming what I can only describe as a "Liberty Evangelist." The Bible says that "he that winneth souls is wise." As believers, we should seek to win the lost, so in a sense, every believer is an evangelist. We can see the parallel and conclude that as Freedom Cell members engaged in the Liberty Movement, we can describe ourselves as Liberty Evangelists.

Another analogy I like to use to describe what it means to be fully committed to the Liberty Movement is that of Johnny Appleseed, who traveled about planting apple seeds. Likewise, Psalm 126 refers to "bearing precious seed." Just as Johnny Appleseed went out to plant apples, and just as believers go out with the precious seed of the truth of God's Word, we can likewise go out as Liberty Evangelists, planting seeds of liberty everywhere we go.

Freedom Cell Survey

Organizing millions of patriots into Freedom Cells and figuring out how to communicate and coordinate our efforts so that we can move as one and speak as one is critically important to the Liberty

Movement, but it won't get very far without a plan. That is why I saw the necessity of writing *The Albert Plan*, and recognized that it had to be bold, comprehensive, and transformational. The Freedom Cell Survey that I have developed is an important tool that we can have in our toolbox for not only getting on the same page as members of Freedom Cells, but also to use in vetting candidates and holding them accountable.

The 2020 Freedom Cell Survey at the back of this book is 100 questions long, and not for the faint of heart. The more questions there are in a comprehensive survey, the more precisely we can collaborate or vet our candidates. Shorter surveys can be very useful, but it is important to have a comprehensive Freedom Cell Survey as a tool in our toolbox.

Freedom Cell Meetings

Members of Freedom Cells will want to enjoy frequent meetings where like-minded patriots gather to discuss the problems that our nation faces and the solutions presented in this plan in order to get on the same page enough to move as one and speak as one. As Ronald Reagan taught us, being in agreement 70% of the time can be a very good starting point for collaborating and aggregating our voices, and our votes.

We should not discard ideas that initially seem to have only limited support, nor should we fight over those issues, but rather we should use those as opportunities for "come let us reason together" discussions. Some out-of-the-box solutions that don't start out with high levels of support may someday turn out to be the transformative changes that we need, so it's important to have an open mind when you attend Freedom Cell meetings.

Each one of us that conducts our own "Campaign of One," is at liberty to gather with a small group of friends or neighbors, or some other affinity group. We can collaborate with other patriots to organize Freedom Cell meetings with dozens, hundreds, or even thousands of Freedom Cell members in any manner that makes sense. We learn best by doing, so the best way to learn what works is to try different meeting formats, sharing our successes with other like-minded patriots.

It is most urgent that We the People demonstrate to liberals that they do not have a monopoly on community organization. We must organize thirty million Americans into Freedom Cells that will empower us to move as one and speak as one, for that is what will strike fear in the hearts of elected officials that have forgotten that they are representatives of their constituents, and not lords over their constituents. In this way we can restore a proper fear of the people by the government, so that we may have liberty.

TRANSFORM THE REPUBLICAN PARTY

Although it is true that the entrenched establishment political class within the Republican Party has consistently ignored, despised and marginalized conservatives, I don't think that the formation of a third party is the solution. There is nothing wrong with the platform of the Republican Party, as it represents the values and beliefs of the majority of Republicans, and that majority is conservative. By taking control of the leadership and the process of the Republican Party, a minority of establishment political class operatives manage to pay lip service to conservative values in order to gain the support of conservatives while pursuing big government policies that are more in line with liberals, statists and globalists than with the values of the conservative majority of the party they represent.

Conservatives are like the Peanuts character Charlie Brown, and the entrenched establishment political class Republicans are like Lucy, always managing to convince Charlie Brown that this time she will somehow keep her promise and hold the football so that Charlie Brown can kick the ball despite the fact that every time she has promised to hold the football for Charlie Brown to kick she has always pulled it away at the last second.

It is time for conservatives to simply take the ball away from the entrenched establishment political class Republicans that have been calling the plays for way too long. We don't have to leave the Republican Party and start a third party. We the People can start a third party *within* the Republican Party by organizing Freedom Cells in every precinct that will overwhelm the RINO Republicans at every level of organization of the Republican Party. In order to take back the Republican Party and keep it, it will take the active focused effort of large numbers of conservative activists that will stay in the game year after year.

The fundamental problem that we face as conservatives is the fact that the vast majority of conservatives are too passive. The failure of conservatives to be politically active is the reason why conservatives do not run the Republican Party. Through being more active in the process, RINO Republicans have a disproportionate share of influence, leading to the selection of candidates that do not reflect the majority conservative view of the party.

There is no way that a third party would ever work unless huge numbers of conservatives become much more active in the political process. If millions of conservatives broke away and started a third party, it would not be long before the majority of the activists that started the party would become too passive, and the elixir of political power will transform sufficient numbers of the movement into members of the entrenched establishment political class, creating just another vehicle for the establishment to commandeer.

Since the problem is a lack of sufficient activism on the part of conservatives, and starting a third party will go nowhere, We the People should get our act together and implement the very clear solution to the problem by getting tens of millions of conservatives to become sufficiently active in the political process to make a real difference. It makes no sense to pursue activism by large numbers of people within a third party before we first try activism by large numbers of people within the Republican Party.

One of the key things that concerned patriotic Americans can do to take our country back and restore the liberties and prosperity that we so desperately desire is to become knowledgeable about the process and mechanics of the Republican Party. Acquiring the knowledge and learning the skills to be involved in party politics is the first step of political activism.

Most people think that activism is voting and perhaps showing up at a rally. Most people think that being involved in local party politics is a waste of time, and is something that only entrenched establishment political types engage in. The extent to which the establishment political class types dominate party politics is determined by the extent to which patriotic freedom loving Americans fail to become involved in the process. We the People can take over the Republican Party if enough patriots become active.

Dominate Party Organization, Rules and Structure

Through the freedom of association guaranteed to us by the First Amendment, We the People have the liberty of forming political parties, which are in essence clubs. How many of us would join a club without knowing the rules? How many of us would join the club without participating in club activities? How many of us would not participate in any of the club activities all year long and then show up at a Christmas party of the club and complain to every member of the club that we speak to about the leadership of the club, the rules of the club and the decisions made by the club throughout the prior year? That would be kind of silly and wrong to do, wouldn't it?

In a similar way, it is silly and wrong for anyone to be completely disengaged from Republican Party activities, even though a registered member of the Republican Party, and then display some of the ignorance, attitudes and misbehavior that we see on display during primary election season. Rather than complain, and endure unsatisfactory results on the back end of the process, the better path is for We the People, in sufficient numbers, to become knowledgeable of and become engaged in the activities of the Republican Party from the grassroots precinct level all the way up to national committee and convention activities. It really isn't that complicated, and it can actually be fun and enlightening!

Precinct Reorganization

Republican Party activities and organization start at the lowest level at which local elections are organized, which most commonly are election precincts. In my limited experience being involved in Republican Party politics, which has been in Greenville County, South Carolina, the Republican Party has what they call precinct reorganizations every two years. The precinct reorganizations are open to all members of the Republican Party, but the members that actually attend the reorganization meetings have the privilege and responsibility of voting for precinct officers, inviting members in attendance to become candidates to serve as delegates to County, district, or state conventions, proposing any resolutions or rules changes to be considered at the county, district, state or national level, and conducting any other business at the precinct level.

It is at the precinct level that We the People must organize ourselves at the grassroots level in order to take back the Republican Party from establishment political class control. Everything else bubbles up from the precinct level, including the advancement of people that may start out with the best of intentions, but eventually become part of the establishment political class. Establishment types are not born that way; they are bred by the system.

I was first introduced to my precinct reorganization when, a few days prior to the scheduled reorganization, a friend of mine in another precinct told me about the reorganization and suggested that I participate. There were only about four or five of us that showed up at the meeting, which was a very informal process that followed the protocols contained in the precinct reorganization packet that one of the others had picked up from the Greenville County Republican Party. There were so few people in attendance that there were more offices to fill than people in attendance.

If We the People will form a Freedom Cell for each precinct, the Freedom Cell can conduct regular meetings as a subset of the precinct similar to the way the Freedom Caucus meets as a subset of the Republican Caucus of the House of Representatives. We the People should form Freedom Cells for each precinct with such overwhelming numbers that at the time of precinct reorganization, the Freedom Cell for each precinct would effectively become the voice for each precinct. With sufficient numbers, Freedom Cell members can easily overwhelm the Republican Party at the precinct level by electing like-minded advocates of *The Albert Plan* to every office and delegate slot available for each precinct.

Of the numerous conceivable affinity groups that transformational conservatives may choose to organize Freedom Cells around, Freedom Cells organized around the local election precinct is one of the most critical ones for Minutemen to participate in. If we are to consolidate and magnify our voice and move as one so that we may take our country back, we must do so at the Republican Party grassroots precinct level. That is where the process starts to elect the right kind of conservative representatives that will stand up to the entrenched establishment political class.

County Meetings and Convention

The next level in the structure and organization of the Republican Party, at least in the state of South Carolina, is at the county level. My precinct, for example, elected a president and an executive committeeman that would attend executive committee meetings of the Greenville County Republican Party every other month. The executive committeeman had the authority to vote at the meetings on behalf of the precinct, with the president of the precinct voting in the absence of the executive committeeman.

When We the People overwhelm the Republican Party at the precinct level and elect representatives to the next level, we will be able to continue to dominate the process through the election of County officers, convention delegates, as well as the process of rulemaking and resolutions that will then bubble up to the next level in the party. The activities of the Greenville County Republican Party, for example, culminate with the county convention.

The county level is where we see establishment political class types in action. We the People will prevail in overwhelming and transforming the Republican Party at the county level if we have Patriot members of Freedom Cells that either have experience with the process or quickly learn the process in order to protect the conservative grassroots movement from being co-opted by entrenched establishment types

District and State Conventions

Just as counties are rolled up into congressional districts for the purpose of elections, the Republican Party is organized with sublevels of activity that culminate with the district convention. Populous cities such as Los Angeles, Chicago or New York City obviously have slightly different structures, as one county may have two or more congressional districts. Entire states like Vermont and Alaska have just one congressional district. Regardless of differences in population density, the structure and organization of the Republican Party follows the same pattern of small election precincts, wards, etc. being rolled up into one or more subgroups that culminate with a congressional district.

In South Carolina, the Republican Party wraps things up with a state convention every two years. Along the way, from precinct to state convention, elections are held for offices and delegates, and decisions are made by voice vote or ballot. The process is a very orderly process most of the time, with parliamentary procedure and parliamentarians used to keep order.

Republican National Committee

At the very top of the food chain of the Republican Party is the Republican National Committee. Predictably, as you go higher up the line from precinct, to county, to congressional district, to state, and then to the national level, the entrenched establishment political class becomes stronger, and the corruption greater. It will take some time, but if We the People are to dominate the Republican Party, we will have to be very organized, diligent and determined in order to displace and repudiate the entrenched establishment political class and to remove establishment types from the state and national levels of the GOP. We can do it in four years if we get organized.

If We the People will show up consistently in overwhelming numbers that demonstrate the sincerity of concern that we have for saving our Republic, we will have no problem following the rules of the Republican Party to transform the Republican Party into one of bright colors, instead of pale pastels, to use the words of President Ronald Reagan.

SIX

The Clamoring

THE SILENT MAJORITY MUST BECOME THE CLAMORING MAJORITY

The strength of the Constitution lies entirely in the determination of each citizen to defend it. Only if every single citizen feels duty-bound to do his share in this defense are the constitutional rights secure.

– Albert Einstein

We the People must restore integrity to federal elections if we are even going to have a chance to save our Republic. The silent majority must become the clamoring majority in order to stop the Marxists that are trying to destroy our Republic, and with it, all of Western civilization.

Restoring election integrity is the seminal issue of our time, for if we do not restore election integrity, we are no longer governed by the consent of the governed, and the United States will become a banana republic. There are many changes that We the People must clamor for, but the most urgent and immediate need is to organize patriots to speak as one and move as one to immediately restore integrity to federal elections.

TO RESTORE ELECTION INTEGRITY

Democrats have been using an "all of the above" strategy to create organized confusion and maximum opportunity to commit election fraud, so We the People must use an "all of the above" strategy to eliminate every conceivable opportunity for election fraud or voter fraud to occur in our federal elections, and then state-by-state we must also restore election integrity to state and local elections.

The Albert Plan to Restore Election Integrity

If we take seriously what Albert Einstein said, that "the strength of the Constitution lies entirely in the determination of each citizen to defend it," we should realize that We the People need not take an oath to defend the Constitution against all enemies, foreign and domestic; we can simply step up and do it. Was Einstein placing the bar too high when he said "only if every single citizen feels duty-bound to do his share in this defense are the constitutional rights secure?"

We the People must not shirk from our responsibility to do our share in the defense of our constitutional rights because there are some among us that are lazy, ignorant, or rightly classified as enemies of the Constitution that make it impossible to meet the 100% participation that Einstein seems to require.

We all have time, talent, and treasure in different measure, which is why *The Albert Plan* calls for every concerned patriot to form or join Freedom Cells, and to participate in a manner that they can sustain for the duration of the battle. All can be Minutemen, but some will be "all in" in the liberty movement.

Freedom Cells are decentralized and distributed self-organizing groups, and as such, can organize in any manner that the members of each group see fit. Freedomcells.com has been set up for each person that joins the website to join the United States group, state groups and congressional district groups in order to be counted, but the real action will be at the precinct, County, State House District and State Senate District levels. Please join these groups where you are registered or eligible to vote, and invite others to do likewise, but don't hesitate to form redundant groups on other platforms because big tech is determined to shut down our opportunities to communicate and organize.

Ultimately, it will take a constitutional amendment to impose election integrity upon liberal states, but We the People must make every effort at the state and federal level to clamor for the following specific elements of election integrity:

1. Decouple federal elections from state & local elections by prohibiting other elections from being held within sixty days of Federal Election Day.
2. Use fingerprints or other biometric means to confirm the legal status of all persons in the United States.
3. Require voter registration by congressional district and voting precinct thirty days prior to a federal election.
4. Require the publication of a list of all eligible voters by congressional district and voting precinct thirty days prior to a federal election.
5. Require in-person voting on Federal Election Day, with no early voting, and very limited absentee voting.
6. Absentee voters cast their ballots in person at authorized polling locations that forward absentee ballots by secure courier to appropriate congressional districts.
7. Voter identity and eligibility is confirmed for each voter at the polling location by photographic ID and fingerprint, or by other biometric means, if the voter has no fingers.
8. Voters cast one paper ballot for each race in a federal election, white for a congressional race, pink for a Senate race, and light blue for a presidential race.
9. Voters affix their thumbprint or fingerprint to the back of each ballot prior to entering the voting booth.
10. The population for each election precinct is limited to 5000 citizens.
11. Ballots are sorted, counted and reported at each election precinct on election night after polls close.
12. Elections at each precinct are conducted with full transparency, with live stream video and the opportunity for the public to observe the voting and counting process from the perimeter of the voting area.
13. Require the publication of a list of all actual voters by congressional district and voting precinct within three days of a federal election.
14. Require the storage of ballots by precinct for one year in a storage facility for each congressional district.
15. Require severe criminal penalty for any intentional matching of the identity of the voter fingerprint on the back of a ballot with the vote cast on the front.

Implementing these fifteen elements of election integrity would eliminate virtually all opportunities for election fraud and voter fraud in federal elections. We the People could then focus on restoring election integrity to each of our home states by clamoring for the implementation of similar elements to state and local elections. State elections could be decoupled from local elections in order to simplify the process and focus the attention of voters on state elections on the first Tuesday after the first Monday in November in odd-numbered years, and local elections at a separate time so that each individual decision by voters could be made on a separate paper ballot.

2020 Election Farce: The Remedy

In the middle of October 2020, I started posting videos to *The Albert Plan* YouTube channel. In Episode 13, which I posted October 27, 2020, about a week before the election, I posed the question about whether it was plausible that President Trump could lose the election, and gave my reasons for believing that the only way that President Trump could plausibly lose the election was by election fraud and voter fraud.

In that video, I expressed my view that the Covid-19 state of emergency was being used by Democrats to commit massive election fraud, and that President Trump had the authority and duty to stop the coup that was in progress by immediately imposing the election integrity measures proposed in this plan upon all states using all of his powers as president and commander-in-chief.

On November 17, 2020, two weeks after the election, I posted *The Albert Plan Episode 19*, entitled *2020 Election Farce: The Remedy* to the channel. In that episode I asserted that President Trump had the duty and authority to declare the 2020 election a failed election, to declare the election null and void, and to require that all election jurisdictions immediately publish the list of eligible voters in their jurisdictions as of November 3, 2020, and that a new federal election be conducted two weeks later using the election integrity measures proposed in this plan, conducted by and under the supervision of the United States military to assure that all states have election integrity.

Shortly before and shortly after the 2020 election, it was my firm belief that in order for the majority of Americans to have faith and confidence in the results of the 2020 election and thereby to have a peaceful transition of power, we needed to conduct a new federal election using the simple election integrity measures that I proposed in those videos and in this book. The way that the election was shaping up, and the way that it was conducted, made it clear to me that We the People were in a lose-lose situation.

As the evidence of massive election fraud was piling up in the weeks after the election, President Trump had the opportunity to recognize that a coup was being perpetrated against our Republic, to declare the election null and void, to seize and audit all ballots, voting machines and any other forensic evidence, and to schedule a new federal election using the common sense election integrity measures proposed in this plan in order to hold a free, fair and transparent election that would have been accepted by the vast majority of Americans of all parties and persuasions.

If President Trump had taken those steps and imposed election integrity upon the entire nation during the Covid-19 emergency, we would have seen the whole truth, and all the evidence showing that the nefarious actors were indeed attempting a coup. For whatever reason, President Trump missed this opportunity to set things right, and we are now in greater distress than our nation has ever seen.

As We the People, the clamoring majority, clamor for common sense election integrity measures to be immediately put in place by our state legislatures so that we may have future federal elections with integrity, we must also clamor for correcting the great wrong perpetrated against our Republic on November 3, 2020. As Steve Bannon says, "It is a wound that will not heal."

It is improbable that we will be able to conduct a new federal election, but if the truth comes out in the full forensic audits conducted by Arizona, and other states that are bold enough to search for the truth, that Joe Biden did not win the presidency, Democrats did not win the Senate, and Democrats did not win a majority in the House of Representatives, perhaps Democrats would accept a new federal election using the election integrity measures proposed in this plan. Sadly, as the party of division, destruction, and death, I believe the Democrats would prefer to see our nation destroyed than to consent to a federal election with integrity because that would expose their fraud.

In the pursuit of an "all of the above" strategy to save our Republic, We the People must simultaneously clamor for restoring integrity to federal elections, as well as for many of the solutions proposed in *The Albert Plan to Save America: 2020 Edition.*

Nullification by States

States should be collectively empowered with the ability to nullify any law, executive order or Supreme Court decision that two thirds of the states find to be objectionable. This will serve as an additional safeguard against overreach by the federal government. A sure way to give the states collectively the right of nullification of federal actions is to do so by constitutional amendment.

Until an amendment establishing that states collectively have the authority to nullify federal actions, and especially during the illegitimate Biden Regime, states should collectively exercise every constitutional authority to nullify, thwart, impede or disrupt every unconstitutional action taken by the federal government. As of the middle of 2021, many states are taking action in this manner.

The Biden Regime threatens action against the natural right of citizens to keep and bear arms, so many states are taking preemptive action by passing constitutional carry laws. Some states, and even counties in liberal states, are establishing Second Amendment sanctuaries. Texas is stepping up to protect the border with Mexico and to build the border wall in order to stem the invasion that has been encouraged by the Biden Regime, and many states are sending law enforcement personnel or national guardsmen to assist in securing our southern border.

Although woefully inadequate, many states have passed measures intended to improve election integrity, and Arizona threatened to arrest federal authorities that try to interfere with the audit of the 2020 election, constitutionally conducted by the Arizona Senate. We the People must clamor for our state legislators to grow a backbone and aggressively pursue every option to nullify or thwart every outlandish action of the Biden Regime.

TO RESTORE NATIONAL SOVEREIGNTY

The single most important function of the federal government that is prescribed by the Constitution is to provide for the common defense. The federal government has been wayward in the execution of this duty, erroneously pursuing redistribution of wealth, social engineering and economic malfeasance instead of performing the single duty that it must not shirk.

Secure Borders

A nation without secure borders is not a sovereign nation. The Biden Regime is compromising national security and is violating the constitutional duty of the federal government to protect the states from invasion. Not only is the Biden regime failing to protect the states from invasion, they are aiding and abetting the invaders! The Biden Regime is in blatant violation of the Constitution.

The United States shall guarantee to every State in this Union a Republican Form of Government, and shall protect each of them against invasion.

– United States Constitution, Article IV, Section 4

We will not continue to exist as a sovereign nation if we don't have secure borders, and have knowledge of and control over the people and goods that enter our country. We the People in every state must clamor for our governors and state legislatures to stand in the gap that has been created by the Biden Regime. Even states controlled by Democrats should feel the heat from We the People to push back against some of the egregious and dangerous actions of the Biden Regime.

Immigration Moratorium

In addition to immediately securing our border, We the People must clamor for an immediate immigration moratorium so that we can fix the problems created by the immigration policies of the last fifty years. The answer to the unprecedented destructive force of virtually unfettered immigration over the past fifty years can be found in the wisdom imparted by Thomas Jefferson, and the example set by Calvin Coolidge in 1924, when immigration was virtually halted for forty years.

Are there no inconveniences to be thrown into the scale against the advantage expected by a multiplication of numbers by the importation of foreigners?

– Thomas Jefferson

Another forty-year immigration moratorium will not fix the problem we have presently with the tens of millions of illegal immigrants that have been invited to violate United States sovereignty. We the People must clamor for requiring biometric identification of all persons in the United States so that we may quickly know the legal status of anyone by a simple fingerprint scan. We must accept fingerprints or facial scans as a God-given means of identification and reject the implementation of microchips that would not only be used for identification, but could be used to track our movements.

With secure borders and the ability to quickly ascertain the legal status of any person, we would be able to immediately deport those who are here illegally that did not register their presence and update their whereabouts, and We the People could sort out what to do with the rest of those who are in the United States illegally.

Those that rushed in after being invited by the Biden Regime would obviously be treated differently than a law-abiding family of four that has been in the United States for twenty years and has teenage children that have assimilated into our culture. Criminals, gang members and members of drug cartels should be immediately deported. United Nations refugees who have not assimilated into our culture should be returned to their home countries or to countries that they would more easily assimilate with.

Withdraw From the United Nations

The United States will not continue to be a sovereign nation if we continue to participate as a member of the United Nations. We must reassert our national sovereignty and reject all efforts by globalists to establish global governance.

The globalist agenda of the United Nations is incompatible with the Constitution of the United States, and the Judeo-Christian values upon which our nation was founded. The freedoms that we enjoy in our constitutional Republic stand in the way of the tyranny of the New World Order that the United Nations globalists seek to establish. The only way that our nation can escape the current globalist path that we are on is if We the People clamor for Congress and our president to completely repudiate the United Nations agenda by immediately withdrawing from the United Nations and expelling them from American soil.

Secure, Strategic Trade

Every sovereign nation should recognize that international trade is, first and foremost, a national security issue. Every nation

111

should pursue their own national interests when seeking to trade with other nations. Each nation should also be strategic in making decisions about trade with other nations.

Free-trade between nations is a myth. Even if free trade among nations were possible, just because the term has the word "free" in it, doesn't make the pursuit of free trade a good thing. Sovereign nations in the pursuit of their own interests will always tinker with any trade arrangements that exist with other sovereign nations. This behavior by sovereign nations should not only be expected, but should be encouraged, as every sovereign nation should be free to engage in activities that advance its own interests.

Absolute free-trade requires not only the successful operation of the free market within the borders of each country; it essentially requires each nation to ignore their own national security and economic strategy, which will effectively erase the borders of each sovereign nation. The dangers of a sovereign nation giving up the security of its borders makes free-trade imprudent, and supports the notion that it is best for nations to abandon the concept of free trade in order to pursue secure, strategic trade. We the People must clamor for secure, strategic trade that puts America first.

TO PREEMPT THE GREAT RESET

The stage is set for globalists to use the impending collapse of the global financial markets as an excuse to introduce their plan to rescue the global markets and to usher in the New World Order that they have been dreaming of for decades. In the summer of 2017, Fed Chairman Janet Yellen stated that she was confident that we would not see another financial crisis in our lifetime.

When we hear such foolishness from the chairman of the entity that has virtually assured that we will see a global financial collapse soon, we can be confident that the collapse is close at hand. We the People must clamor for the Gordian-knot cutting solutions proposed in *The Albert Plan* in order to preempt The Great Reset.

Abolish the Fed and Fractional Banking

Our founders warned us against establishing national, or central banks, for they recognized the potential for the abuse of power by those controlling entities that create money. As the advocates for decentralized and distributed power, and maximum transparency, our founders were prescient in the wisdom they displayed in the founding of our constitutional Republic.

I believe that banking institutions are more dangerous to our liberties than standing armies.

– Thomas Jefferson

History records that the money changers have used every form of abuse, intrigue, deceit, and violent means possible to maintain their control over governments by controlling money and its issuance.

– James Madison

The mandate given by Congress to the Federal Reserve, as modified by the Federal Reserve act of 1977, charged the Fed with the dual role of seeking maximum employment while maintaining stable prices and moderate long-term interest rates. Instead of trusting the free market to create jobs, establish prices and set interest rates, Congress entrusted the Fed with somewhat dubious monetary policy tools to pursue sometimes conflicting goals of maximum employment and low inflation.

Central banks erroneously believe that all deflation is bad, when in fact there are two types of deflation, one that is good for the economy and one that is bad for the economy. Bad deflation results from a dramatic and sustained drop in demand. The deflation experienced during the Great Depression was an example of bad deflation. Good deflation results from the gradual, steady increase in production relative to consumption, which increases sup-

113

ply relative to demand, thereby reducing prices. Bad deflation will generally result in the decline of the average standard of living, while good deflation will generally result in an improvement in the average standard of living.

In a free market that is substantially unfettered from government intervention, most people will work and contribute to real economic output because God wired us to work. God instructed man to work and to have dominion over the world that we live in. The Bible also instructs us to provide for our own needs and the needs of others, and admonishes that those capable of working that will not work should not eat.

If everyone who is capable of working was free to work and was also deprived of any opportunity to enjoy having their living expenses met by the labor of other hard-working people, we would see aggregate production increase substantially. Good deflation would naturally occur, resulting in an improvement in the average standard of living.

The reason that our economy does not enjoy an increasing average standard of living and enjoy the benefits of good deflation is because government policy restricts the opportunity of Americans to freely produce more output and enjoy the fruit of their labor, and because government policy has created the opportunity for tens of millions of American citizens and millions of illegal immigrants to consume far more than they produce. The flawed economic policy of the federal government has negated the natural deflationary force of the free market to the detriment of most Americans.

The Federal Reserve policy of pursuing a target inflation rate of 2% instead of permitting a natural deflation rate of about 2% to occur has led to the destruction of the middle class, and has also deprived lower income Americans of the opportunity to enjoy economic prosperity. Inflation is a hidden tax. In thirty-five years prices double at a nominal inflation rate of 2%, whereas prices would be cut in half in the same period of time with a nominal deflation rate of 2%, resulting in a four times difference in price. We the People must clamor for a constitutional amendment to abolish the Federal Reserve and fractional banking, which permits banks to create money out of thin air.

When we abolish the Federal Reserve, Congress would resume its authority to create money, but should pursue a sound money policy. Government has the responsibility to provide its citizens with sound money that is of stable value and has integrity. Governments that do not fulfill this responsibility put their citizens and nation at risk.

Government should supply adequate currency, whether physical or electronic, to support the level of economic activity that the free market generates. Government should not use money or monetary policy to control interest rates, inflation rates or the availability of credit. The free market is more efficient and more equitable in these matters, and has no political agenda. Rather than permit Congress the opportunity to create unlimited quantities of currency, We the People should force Congress to pursue sound money policy by constitutional amendment.

Congress shall issue no more than $2000 in coin, paper or electronic currency for every ounce of gold held in reserve, and shall not redeem currency for gold or deplete reserves of gold for any reason.

– Proposed Constitutional Amendment Language

Year of Jubilee

Instead of allowing those that created the crisis to "solve" the crisis, We the People should choose liberty instead and reject the New World Order that globalists wish to impose upon us. We should reject central banking and the centralized control of the global financial system by globalists, and make a bold move in restoring our political and economic freedoms. We the People have the option of choosing which chaotic path we take, one that brings a New World Order out of a global financial collapse, or one that intentionally collapses the global financial system in order to restore economic and personal liberty.

> *The modern theory of the perpetuation of debt has drenched the earth with blood, and crushed its inhabitants under burdens ever accumulating.*

– Thomas Jefferson

When We the People successfully preempt the coming reset of the global financial system by abolishing the Federal Reserve and fractional banking, we will see a collapse of asset prices. The immediate collapse of asset prices and the natural deflationary forces that will kick in once prices have stabilized at a new equilibrium will result in a dramatic redistribution of wealth toward debtholders, unless debt balances are indexed down or completely eliminated.

Any mechanism by which debts are indexed down by some measure that equitably reflects the collapse in asset prices will lag behind the collapse in prices, creating uncertainty in the marketplace that may create an impediment to the full throttle operation of the economy.

Since worldwide debt escalated dramatically in the last fifteen years, and there seems to be no end to the debt binge that the United States has been on for decades, it seems that it is time that we face the fact that our nation is bankrupt. We should encourage other nations to join with us in dealing with the staggering problem of worldwide debt. The debt problem can be dealt with more completely and decisively if other industrialized nations will join with us in slaying that dragon.

We have at our disposal the option of employing a one-time solution of simultaneously declaring national bankruptcy, and declaring a Year of Jubilee, whereby all debts are canceled or converted to equity. In order to avoid future debt bubbles, we should also take the additional step of outlawing debt altogether, or establishing that every twenty-five years there will be another Year of Jubilee when all debts that have accrued by that time are canceled.

Since the escalation of global debt has occurred without a substantial change in wealth worldwide, that escalation in debt has simply redistributed the claims to worldwide wealth, concentrating wealth more and more in the hands of fewer individuals and corporations. Declaring a Year of Jubilee whereby all debt is canceled or converted to equity will indeed redistribute wealth, as debtors will see their wealth increase at the expense of creditors. Part of that redistribution of wealth would reverse the redistribution of wealth that occurred with the escalation of debt.

Since any reset of the global financial system will necessarily create winners and losers through massive redistribution of wealth, and any massive redistribution of wealth will occur in an inequitable fashion, we should structure the eradication of debt in a manner that creates the greatest potential for economic revival while also achieving reasonable equity.

In *The Albert Plan to Save America: 2020 Edition*, I provide more details on how We the People can clamor for a Year of Jubilee to skew the benefits in favor of the bottom 90% of Americans in order to assure a smooth transition, as well as how we can clamor for breaking the stranglehold that Wall Street has on financial markets.

TRUST-BUSTING

President Teddy Roosevelt was known as a "trustbuster" when he ushered in an era of antitrust legislation that broke up many of the cartels that big businesses had established to control many segments of the economy in the early twentieth century. We the People must clamor for a new era of trustbusting to break up the numerous cartels that have developed over the last fifty years. There is a greater need now than there was a century ago to take on the cartels, and that includes the federal government cartel.

Breaking up the Big Tech Cartel

The 2020 Election Farce and its aftermath exposed the bias in the influence of the big tech cartel. They have been involved in influencing the elections and they have censored free speech by conservatives with impunity. There is an unholy alliance between big government and big tech, so We the People must demand that state and federal legislatures take on big tech.

We must take an "all the above" strategy to slay this dragon before it consumes the last vestiges of liberty. Section 230 protections of big tech must be eliminated. Big tech companies must be broken up. Some technologies should be deemed utilities and regulated as such. Our means of communication have changed, and the town square has evolved to a point where if big tech is allowed to continue on its course, we will lose the ability to have our voices heard.

Another way to reign in big tech is to require tech companies to provide users with an easy to find and easy to use dashboard where users could select options such as retaining rights to their content, denying the use of cookies, blocking all advertisements, blocking the sharing of any user information, requiring that the platform retain no memory of any user activity that would influence a search by the user, and any other option that users could select that would protect consumer property and privacy.

Such a user dashboard would not only protect the privacy and property rights of users, it would force big tech companies to start charging users that opt out of all of the means by which big tech companies exploit value from users. Facebook might have to reevaluate their commitment to always being a free service.

Big tech should also be broken up in more traditional ways by requiring companies to divest from certain operations that reduce competition. Google should be required to sell YouTube. Facebook should be required to sell Instagram. Amazon should be broken up by having them divest of companies like CreateSpace, which was anticompetitive in the self-publishing market, and they should be required to spin off their distribution and logistics business, making it accessible to companies that compete against Amazon in the online retail business. Amazon has used its distribution and logistics to create illegal tying arrangements where vendors and customers have to buy or sell products with delivery services as a package deal. Apple and Google should have to sell off their app stores.

Federal law should prohibit big tech companies from censoring, blocking, or hindering the activities of users based upon political views or opinions, and should provide stiff penalties that users can avail themselves of to quickly assess damages against big tech companies that trample upon the free speech of users.

If corporate campaign donations are prohibited, big tech should be required to tiptoe through the political realm for fear of violating federal campaign lines. Mark Zuckerberg would be free to donate billions of dollars to individual campaigns if he wanted to, but Facebook would be banned from making direct or indirect campaign contributions.

There is an urgent need for modern-day trust-busting to take place to break up numerous cartels. Big tech isn't the only cartel that needs to be broken up. In addition to big tech, we have Big Government, Big Business, Big Labor, Big Medicine, Big Pharma, Big Banks, Big Insurance, Big Education, and any other cartel that has become too big and too powerful to be good for America.

Breaking up the Wall Street Cartel

For decades I have believed that investment options on Wall Street have been essentially funneling too large a share of investable dollars into too few options. SEC regulations have made it next to impossible for small entrepreneurs to raise money directly from investors. With the advent of block chain technology, which enables something like bitcoin to exist, we finally have an opportunity to unshackle entrepreneurs from the constraints imposed by the unholy alliance of big government and big business.

Like most solutions proposed in *The Albert Plan*, the solution is simple, but not easy, for implementing the simple solution would completely disrupt global financial markets, and would make the implementation of The Great Reset by global elites much more difficult. True liberty is decentralized and distributed, just like block chain technology, which is why it would be so appropriate to use block chain technology to bring greater liberty for small investors to invest directly in small business ventures.

Crypto currencies are enabled by block chain technology; they are not synonymous with block chain technology. I don't think I would ever recommend investing in crypto currencies, but I am grateful that the model that we see in crypto currencies can be used to introduce a new stock exchange that is not regulated by the SEC, because SEC regulation simply is not necessary.

Investment platforms like Robin Hood, Schwab and TD Ameritrade have shown that trading stocks can be done at little or no cost. Block chain technology can be used to track ownership of shares at negligible cost. Instead of seeing thousands of crypto currencies pop up, we should empower entrepreneurs to raise money through block chain enabled shares of stock that would be sold for real dollars, and those dollars invested by the entrepreneurs. People would be buying shares of a real corporation instead of shares of a crypto currency without tangible value. Ordinary investors could invest in new companies without having to wait for investment banks and venture capitalists to reap most of the value created by the new entity.

Even with SEC regulation, big corporations have defrauded investors of billions, so caveat emptor should be adequate protection for the small investor to invest his own hard-earned money in a venture that he believes in without government interference. Eliminating SEC regulation and using current technologies for trading and tracking ownership of shares would open the floodgates for entrepreneurs to raise capital to build businesses, and would also help break up the Wall Street cartel. We the People should clamor for decentralized and distributed financial markets.

The elimination of the double taxation of dividends would allow people to enjoy greater anonymity in their financial dealings because corporations would pay dividends with after-tax dollars, which would require no accountability for who owns the shares.

Some of the other proposals in *The Albert Plan*, when implemented, will also contribute to breaking up the Wall Street cartel. A flat tax on all income regardless of source, and the elimination of all deductions and preferences would remove the golden handcuffs that current tax laws place on investors. There would be no incentive to hold shares of stock for over a year in order to enjoy a lower capital gains tax rate. There would be no preference for tax-free municipal bonds. The implementation of free-market healthcare would no longer tie health insurance to employment, which would liberate people to change jobs or to start their own businesses.

All of the cartels, of course, will fight vigorously to keep the ideas presented in *The Albert Plan* from gaining traction. It is up to We the People to fight harder and in greater numbers to save our Republic and to secure our personal and economic liberty.

DECOUPLING FROM CHINA

Whether or not Covid-19 was developed in a lab, or was intentionally released, the way that the Chinese Communist Party covered up the existence, severity and characteristics of the disease and withheld information that could have saved countless lives around the world is reason enough for the United States and all other freedom loving nations to decouple from China. China should be recognized as a pariah state by freedom loving nations.

This new reason to decouple from China is merely the newest of a long, growing list of reasons why the United States should take immediate and decisive action to unwind all of the entanglements that we have gotten ourselves into with a country that behaves like our arch nemesis. China has been waging economic warfare against the United States for decades. They boast about unrestricted warfare against the United States giving them superiority in the very near future. We the People should clamor for our federal government, our states, and especially U.S. companies to immediately take action to decouple from China.

FREE MARKET EDUCATION

When I published *The Albert Plan to Save America: 2020 Edition* in June 2020, I included a chapter entitled Free-Market Education in which I laid out the case for eliminating government involvement in education and empowering parents to fulfill their God-given responsibility to educate their own children. The way that the Biden Regime has been pushing vaccinations of schoolchildren, mask-wearing by children as young as two years old, and the promotion of Critical Race Theory has created an even more urgent need for We the People to clamor to get government completely out of the education of our children. The pushback by parents of all political persuasions is one of the blessings of government overreach.

The federal government has no business being in education, as it falls outside of the enumerated powers granted to the federal government by the Constitution. It is up to We the People in each of our states to determine if we will tolerate our state governments continuing to be involved in the education of our children. The education function of the public education system has failed to educate our children because the focus has been on the indoctrination function of public schools. This is something that parents should not tolerate.

We the People must clamor for the federal government to extract itself from education, but the most direct route for us to cut the Gordian-knot is to clamor for each of our states to stop taking education dollars from the federal government, and to immediately take steps to dismantle the state public education system.

If the citizens of any state will clamor loudly and consistently enough to embolden their state legislatures to take the bold move of pursuing free-market education, states could do so quite simply by making direct payments of $5000 per year per child to parents for the education of their children, with no strings attached.

The free market will spring into action, creating a multitude of options for providing our children with a better education at lower cost. States could reduce the education voucher for each child by 5% every year, as the free market will drive the cost of education down even more quickly.

It's great that parents are waking up and clamoring before school boards about vaccinations and Critical Race Theory, but the public education system is irredeemably broken, which is okay, because there is a better way. The clamoring for free-market education should be attractive to all parents and grandparents regardless of political affiliation. We the People simply have to get the job done.

FREE MARKET HEATHCARE

In 1960, healthcare costs were about 5% of GDP, but today healthcare costs are approaching 20% of GDP. Why is that? When you look at all of the goods and services produced by the United States economy, it makes no sense that healthcare costs amount to anywhere close to 20% of our gross domestic product. Healthcare prices are obviously distorted, and not set by free-market price discovery. The dramatic escalation in healthcare costs is a direct result of the fact that we have a third-party payer system whereby almost all healthcare costs are paid for by government or insurance companies, and not by patients.

Government involvement in the healthcare system leads to higher costs. Instead of increasing government involvement to eventually move to a single-payer system leading to lower quality healthcare at higher cost, if we get the government out of the equation and eliminate health insurance as an option, we will then have a single-payer system where the single-payer is the patient in each healthcare transaction.

Free-market healthcare will permit our healthcare system to thrive and innovate, meeting the needs of patients and providing all those employed in the healthcare system with the satisfaction of helping others, while making a reasonable living without the burden of interference by government and insurance companies making their jobs more difficult and less fulfilling.

If there was a way to salvage Obamacare, it would then be necessary to outlaw employer provided health insurance plans in order to permit the portability of plans and to correct the damage done to small business. Giving big business an unfair advantage in procuring lower cost large group health insurance plans makes it more difficult for small businesses to attract quality employees in order to compete with big business. Small business is where most jobs are created, and if we continue to allow insurance companies to sell health insurance policies, we would need to fix this problem. The problem goes away if we repeal Obamacare and outlaw health insurance policies.

The involvement of insurance companies and the government in making third-party payments for prescription drugs, particularly under Obamacare, leads to artificially high drug prices. Drug companies are able to engage in price gouging, because under the current broken system, doctors are afraid to not prescribe medication, and insurance companies are virtually required to provide the medication, no matter what the cost is. One thing is certain, if We the People implement free-market healthcare by eliminating health insurance and government payments, the free market will permit nowhere near the pricing that drug companies are currently able to extract from third-party payers. The Big Pharma cartel will lose their opportunity to price gouge.

Insurance companies and the health insurance policies that they sell do nothing to improve healthcare or add value to the healthcare system. The basic function of health insurance is to spread the risk of the financial burden of unanticipated healthcare events, which is something that we can collectively do without any involvement of insurance companies. We the People now have the opportunity to insist that our government permit us to spread the risk of catastrophic healthcare events in a much more cost-effective and equitable manner.

The most direct path to getting the federal government out of the healthcare market is to transfer Medicaid and Medicare to the states, repeal Obamacare, and outlaw health insurance. States that pursue the full implementation of *The Albert Plan* will then eliminate Medicaid and Medicare and any other involvement by the state in the healthcare market in their state in order to permit free-market healthcare to complete the transformation of the healthcare system. States that do not embrace the magnitude and direction of this plan for free-market healthcare will have much difficulty controlling healthcare costs.

The Free-Market Healthcare chapter in *The Albert Plan to Save America: 2020 Edition* goes into much more detail about the rationale for getting third-party payers out of our healthcare system and how free-market healthcare would be implemented. One new idea that makes sense is to eliminate patent protection on medications and medical devices and establishing a Nobel Peace Prize style way of rewarding healthcare innovations.

The Canadian doctors that invented insulin set a good example when they gave away the patent on insulin so that it would be available to people at very nominal cost. The current cost of insulin illustrates just how broken our healthcare system is, because the costs have escalated under the third-party payers system. The profit motive is not the only reason for healthcare innovations, so removing patent protection may give us great benefits without diminishing healthcare innovation too much. The Nobel Prize approach would add additional incentive without driving up costs for patients.

FREE MARKET ENERGY

For decades, United States energy policy has been dictated by radical environmentalists and crony capitalists. The Washington cartel has given lip service to the idea of the United States achieving energy independence while pursuing policies that make energy independence impossible.

Just when the United States became energy independent under President Trump, the Biden Regime wasted no time in setting our country back by canceling U.S. pipelines and oil leases on federal lands, and giving the green light to a pipeline from Russia to Europe. We the People must clamor for the changes necessary to unleash the domestic production of abundant, cheap energy that will unleash free-market capitalism. We must embrace an "all of the above" energy policy in order to pursue free-market energy.

Energy is the lifeblood of economic activity, so the United States cannot afford to jeopardize national security and economic liberty by continuing our dependence upon foreign sources of oil or by experimenting with expensive emerging technologies that are not yet economically viable or scalable for generating energy. We must pursue all viable energy options without picking winners and losers. We must stop subsidizing new technologies and penalizing energy sources that we relied upon to build our nation.

SEVEN

The Clamoring: Part 2

DEMOCRATS DON'T HAVE A MONOPOLY ON COMMUNITY ORGANIZATION

If the federal government should overpass the just bounds of its authority and make a tyrannical use of its powers, the people, whose creature it is, must appeal to the standard they have formed, and take such measures to redress the injury done to the Constitution as the exigency may suggest and prudence justify.

– Alexander Hamilton, Federalist number 33

Getting tens of millions of patriots to get on the same page and clamor to restore election integrity is the best path forward for We the People to speak as one and move as one toward the point on the horizon that will save our Republic. There are many elements of *The Albert Plan to Save America: 2020 Edition* that We the People must also simultaneously clamor for. We need more than a three point plan; we need a bold, comprehensive, transformational plan to restore federalism, to restore national sovereignty, to restore individual liberty, to restore limited government, and to unleash free-market capitalism.

TO RESTORE FEDERALISM

Many of the issues that divide our nation could be peacefully re-solved by restoring the division of power between the state and federal governments given to us by the founders. If We the People get the federal government out of education, welfare, housing, labor and other functions that properly belong to the states, each state could differentiate itself from other states by adopting liberal or conservative policies that its citizens want. Perhaps it is time to use a tool that our founders gave us to restore federalism.

Convention of States

The Framers of the Constitution provided for two mechanisms by which amendments to the Constitution may be proposed. The first mechanism, which requires a two-thirds vote by both houses of Congress, is not likely to be used any time soon to propose amendments to limit the powers of the federal government.

The second mechanism for proposing amendments to the Constitution, which is initiated by the states, was designed by the framers to give the states equal opportunity to propose amendments to the Constitution. This mechanism was designed to protect us from a federal government that would be reluctant to introduce amendments limiting the power of that federal government.

The tyranny of the federal government necessitates that we consider quite a few amendments in order to restore the balance of power. We the People desperately need to compel thirty-four of our state legislatures to put Congress on notice that we are calling for a Convention of States to Propose Amendments. The States should not tolerate any delay by Congress or any attempt by Congress to control the process.

We the People, as citizens of our respective states, must engage our state legislators in discussing any and all amendments that should be considered. We should direct our legislatures to engage in discussions with other states about any and all amendments that should be considered. We the People must demand that our legislatures force the hand of Congress and give Congress no option but to call a Convention of States to Propose Amendments.

Although I generally support the Convention of States Project (COSP), I'm concerned that the limited scope that they are calling for will be successfully challenged as unconstitutional, and their limited scope does not include proposing an amendment to protect life from conception until natural death, or a marriage amendment that would affirm God's definition of marriage as between a man and a woman, or even an election integrity amendment desperately needed to restore election integrity in all states.

If We the People are to restore federalism by returning power to the states and the people that has been usurped by the federal government, then we must use an Article V Convention of States to Propose Amendments in order to do so. The mere initiation of that process will focus so much more attention by the citizens of each state on the power vested in each state legislature, it will awaken a movement to elect transformational conservatives to those offices by a more informed electorate that will hold them to account.

Holding Senators and Congressmen Accountable

The Seventeenth Amendment, which provided for the direct election of Senators by the general population of each state, may have sounded like a good idea at the time, but has turned out to be very damaging to our country. We the People should clamor for the repeal of the seventeenth amendment.

The Senate has become an exclusive club with far too much power, little transparency and virtually no accountability. Senators are not accountable enough to the people of the states they are supposed to represent, and are very difficult to remove from office. They are more concerned about preserving their own power and prospects for reelection than they are about the interests of the states that they represent. They have become the very core of the entrenched establishment political class, thumbing their noses with impunity at the people that they represent.

The seventeenth Amendment to the Constitution of the United States is hereby repealed. The authority of the legislatures of the several States to remove Senators from office is hereby affirmed.

– Proposed Constitutional Amendment Language

Recall of Senators

Until such time as We the People are successful in repealing the Seventeenth Amendment, we can mitigate the damage done to our republic by the entrenched establishment political class types that are part of the Senate country club created by the Seventeenth Amendment. Presently, there is no mechanism by which the people, the legislature, or the governor of any state can remove a senator from office, other than by defeating incumbent senators at the ballot box, which is very difficult. We the People should clamor to change that by constitutional amendment.

The citizens of each of the several states may recall a United States Senator representing their state if registered voters in that state sign a recall petition in numbers equal to or greater than ten percent of the number of votes cast during the last senatorial election. A recall election shall be held within sixty days of the certification of the recall petition, and if a majority of voters in the recall election vote to remove the Senator, such removal shall take immediate effect.

– Proposed Constitutional Amendment Language

Recall of Congressmen

Many of the proposals to restore federalism in *The Albert Plan* involve the transfer of power from the federal government back to the states, but it is important to transfer power directly back to the people, when possible. Short of term limits, nothing will check the unbridled lust for power that some members of Congress have than for the people to have a mechanism by which they may recall their member of Congress when they forget who they serve.

The citizens of each congressional district of the several states may recall a Member of the House of Representatives representing their district if registered voters in that district sign a recall petition in numbers equal to or greater than ten percent of the number of votes cast during the last congressional election. A recall election shall be held within sixty days of the certification of the recall petition, and if a majority of voters in the recall election vote to remove the Member of Congress, such removal shall take immediate effect.

– Proposed Constitutional Amendment Language

TO RESTORE INDIVIDUAL LIBERTY

When establishing the American experiment, our founders boldly asserted that all of mankind has been blessed by God with natural rights that cannot be taken away.

We hold these Truths to be self-evident, that all Men are created equal, that they are endowed by their Creator with certain unalienable Rights, that among these are Life, Liberty, and the Pursuit of Happiness–

– Declaration of Independence

The assertion that all people have natural rights, and the acknowledgment of God as the source of those rights is the basis for what I believe is a special obligation that the United States has to promote liberty and resist tyranny throughout the world. The fact that our founding fathers used the words "among these" before listing the specific unalienable rights of life, liberty, and the pursuit of happiness raises the question of what the other natural rights are that our founders may have had in mind at the time of the writing of the Declaration of Independence.

At this time, when the Democrat party, the party of division, destruction and death, is doing its utmost to bring the American experiment to an end, We the People must recommit to the ideals of our founding fathers, and even double down on those ideals by having "Natural Rights Conferences" to discuss the open question of the full list of natural rights with which we have been endowed

131

by God, and what our obligation is as Americans to help citizens of the nations of the world to enjoy the opportunity of experiencing those same natural rights.

Many additional natural rights were asserted in the Constitution or the Bill of Rights, such as the natural right to keep and bear arms, the natural right to freedom of speech, freedom of religion, freedom of assembly, and freedom of association.

Our founders additionally asserted the natural right for We the People to collectively petition the government for a redress of grievances, or to alter a tyrannical government. Embedded in the founding documents is the natural right to own and enjoy property, and to enjoy privacy and the freedom from unreasonable searches and seizures.

All men are created equally free and independent, and have certain inherent rights, of which they cannot, by any compact, deprive or divest their posterity; among which are the enjoyment of life and liberty, with the means of acquiring and possessing property, and pursuing the obtaining of happiness and safety.

– George Mason

It wasn't necessary at the time of the founding of the American experiment, but today it is necessary to assert the obvious natural right to marry without the necessity of a license from the government, or to divorce without the necessity of a decree by the government. We the People have liberty to come together and have "come let us reason together" discussions in order to compile a complete list of the natural rights that all people around the world should be free to enjoy.

We the People must clamor for the federal government, and government at all levels, to restore individual liberty. In *The Albert Plan to Save America: 2020 Edition*, I make numerous proposals to restore personal and economic liberty to Americans.

Life Amendment

We must amend the Constitution to recognize that life begins at conception, and that each life is entitled to protection from the moment of conception until the moment of death from natural causes. Abortion, assisted suicide, and euthanasia should be illegal in this country, just as murder is illegal. All life is precious, and should be protected. The strong should protect the weak. The healthy should protect the infirm. The living should protect the unborn.

> *Recognizing that life begins at conception, the individual rights of each person, from conception to natural death, shall be afforded equal protection under the law.*

– Proposed Constitutional Amendment Language

We the People must clamor for protection of all life from conception until natural death. In the Roe v Wade decision it was made clear that if the personhood of the baby in the womb was established, it would have resulted in a different decision by the court. We need not wait for a constitutional amendment to correct the problem nationwide before we move as one and speak as one in clamoring to our state legislatures to recognize the personhood of the baby in the womb and to outlaw abortion in each state.

Open or Concealed-Carry Amendment

As mentioned earlier, some states or counties have established Second Amendment sanctuaries, passed constitutional carry laws, or removed some of the infringements upon our natural right to keep and bear arms. What I have proposed in *The Albert Plan* is an amendment that would remove all infringements on our right to keep and bear arms nationally with the exception of venues established by Congress that would require sufficient armed personnel within those adequately secured venues.

The individual right to keep and bear arms, whether openly or concealed, shall not be infringed except in venues, established by Congress, which are adequately secured and protected by sufficient armed law enforcement personnel. The individual right to keep and bear arms, whether openly or concealed, shall not be infringed by the imposition of any tax, limit on quantity, permit, license or registration.

– Proposed Constitutional Amendment Language

We the People must drown out the liberal drumbeat to further infringe upon our Second Amendment rights by demanding that our state and federal governments remove infringements upon our right to keep and bear arms that have been incrementally imposed upon us over the years. The Second Amendment alone should have been adequate to keep states from infringing upon our natural right to keep and bear arms, but many liberal states have been successful in infringing upon those rights.

The language of my proposed amendment is intended to permit citizens to keep and bear arms uniformly throughout the country. Anyone traveling from state to state should not have to worry about whether they are violating restrictive gun laws in the states through which they travel. There should be no license, registration or tax imposed on guns and ammunition. The right to keep and bear arms, just like the right to vote, should be limited to United States citizens only.

Our veterans should not be deprived of their Second Amendment rights without due process. A diagnosis of PTSD should not bar any veteran from the right to keep and bear arms. The mentally ill should not lose their right to keep and bear arms; they should be institutionalized if they are a danger to themselves or others. Even criminals that have been deemed to have paid their debt to society should not be deprived of their Second Amendment rights after serving their time and being released from prison.

We the People must use an "all of the above" strategy to clamor for each state to remove all infringements upon our right to keep and bear arms, and to clamor for the federal government to remove all restrictions. The Second Amendment does not give us the right to keep and bear arms; it simply affirmed our natural right to keep and bear arms and stated that those rights "shall not be infringed." The issue should not be up for discussion. Any amendment that were to infringe on our natural right to keep and bear arms would go against the very founding of our nation, but any amendment that clearly removes any current infringements would be acceptable, as it should end those infringements permanently.

Abolish Taxes on all Property

The right to own private property is essential to the existence and continuation of a free society. Property is not truly owned if government has the authority to tax that property. We the People must clamor for a constitutional amendment that prohibits taxation of property, but we must simultaneously clamor within our individual states for the abolition of taxes on property.

No tax shall be levied or collected against any real, personal or financial property, or against the estate of any individual upon death.

– Proposed Constitutional Amendment Language

Eliminating the authority for government at any level to tax property in any form, and limiting the federal government to raising revenue by taxing income and transactions at reasonable levels will unleash a period of unprecedented economic growth. States that abolish property taxes and simultaneously eliminate public education will see a boom in housing and job creation. The mere ownership of property should not trigger tax by any level of government, and we should be free to accumulate wealth and pass it on without the assessment of estate taxes.

135

Eliminate the Minimum Wage

Democrats always seem to advocate for increasing the minimum wage in order to help the poor. The truth is that the minimum wage actually hurts poor people and young people by killing jobs. As is often the case with government policy, the actual impact of the policy is the opposite of the stated intent.

The federal government has no business tinkering with wages and prices. Even if it was a permissible function of the federal government, the free market is more reliable in establishing appropriate prices and wages than any government is capable of doing. States will also do well to respect the free market system by refraining from establishing minimum wages or controlling prices.

We the People must clamor for government at all levels to stop tinkering with the operation of the free market and acting like it is the role of government to create jobs in the first place. The role of government is to ensure the liberty and security of its citizens, and to simply get out of the way of the free market. Minimum wages, the imposition of overtime requirements, price controls and regulations hurt job creators and those that would like to work.

Right to Work Amendment

At the turn of the twentieth century, unions were instrumental in addressing many problems created by big business, but they have changed from advocating for the working man to exploiting the working man. Big Union Cartels have used compulsory union dues to raise money for the Democrat party, and in turn, the Democrat Party has feathered the nests of union leaders.

The Constitution grants Americans the right to assemble, which includes the right to associate with unions for collective bargaining purposes. Each worker should be free to choose whether to join a union or not, whether to associate with a union or to not associate with a union. Compulsory union membership and compulsory union dues should be banned by amendment.

There is a right to work movement that is slowly spreading across the nation, state by state. States are passing right to work laws that effectively end compulsory union membership or dues. States that have passed right to work laws and are permitting the free market to function more freely in other ways are seeing their economies improve. We the People should clamor to accelerate the process and give workers in all states the freedom to work without being compelled to join unions and pay dues that support activities that are contrary to their values and beliefs.

TO RESTORE LIMITED GOVERNMENT

In *The Albert Plan to Save America: 2020 Edition*, I propose several amendments to limit the power of the federal government. We the People should clamor for such amendments, but we should also clamor for each of our states to make any changes within each state that will make incremental progress toward the goal.

Income Tax Amendment

The Democrat mantra that everyone should pay their "fair share" of taxes usually means that the middle class bears the brunt of taxes paid. We the People should clamor for a flat income tax not to exceed 15% on all income from all sources paid by everyone regardless of level of income. There should be no preferences, no deductions, no alternative minimum tax calculations, essentially no complications whatsoever. Corporations should pay the same rate, and there should be no double taxation on dividends of income distributed by corporations that has already been taxed. Such a flat income tax should be implemented at the same time that payroll taxes are eliminated.

All personal and corporate income shall be taxed at the same rate, and shall not exceed fifteen percent.

– Proposed Constitutional Amendment Language

Sales Tax Amendment

When the Sixteenth Amendment to the Constitution regarding the income tax was proposed, it is my understanding that there was great opposition to setting a cap of 15%. It was argued that the federal government would gravitate quickly to that level, as Congress would interpret the cap as permission to elevate the tax rate to that level. If only they had included the provision for a 15% maximum rate in the amendment!

Many have argued for the implementation of a national sales tax as part of a plan for tax reform. It would be an excellent way to simplify tax policy in an efficient, equitable manner, so long as there is a limit to all tax rates and the overall federal tax burden.

My proposal for a simple flat tax on all income at a maximum rate of 15% coupled with a maximum national sales tax of 5% would provide adequate revenue to a properly functioning federal government. The only way to assure that maximum tax rates are established is to do so by constitutional amendment. It is important to note that this proposed amendment does not establish a national sales tax; it simply sets an upper limit on any future national sales tax rate.

Any national sales tax, if implemented, shall not exceed 5%, and no value added tax shall be imposed without amendment.

– Proposed Constitutional Amendment Language

If we restore the power to the states and to the people that has been usurped by the federal government, and if we limit the role of the federal government to activities prescribed by the Constitution, the federal government should be able to function effectively with revenue at well below the total of the maximum permitted income tax rate of 15% and the maximum permitted sales tax rate of 5%. The full implementation of *The Albert Plan* would result in a dramatic reduction in federal expenditures, and a doubling of real

GDP within ten years. The federal government should eventually be able to function with a flat income tax rate of 12%, using a national sales tax sparingly in order to balance the budget.

The beauty of incorporating the use of a national sales tax with a low flat tax on income is that the sales tax rate can be immediately adjusted as needed with instantaneous results, and virtually no cost of administration. A disciplined Congress that is accountable to the people would be able to adjust the sales tax upwards as needed and then quickly reduce the rate when the need has been met. We the People need to be diligent in holding Congress accountable and making our voices heard when they are slow to make appropriate changes to taxes, spending, or policy.

One of the big benefits of having a flat tax coupled with a sales tax is that any change in the income tax rate or the sales tax rate will be equitable. We will remove the opportunity for the entrenched establishment political class to use revenue as a mechanism for the redistribution of wealth. The full implementation of *The Albert Plan* will dismantle the expenditure side of the redistribution of wealth scheme that the entrenched establishment political class has used for decades to acquire power and control.

When We the People make revenue generation at the federal level simple and equitable, and we eliminate federal spending that the federal government should not be engaged in, sad establishment types that have lost their levers of control will flock to state and local governments. We the People must also make diligent effort to take our state and local governments back from the entrenched establishment political class, and clamor for changes of similar magnitude and direction as those proposed in *The Albert Plan*.

Balanced Budget Amendment

Contrary to what proponents of Modern Monetary Theory say, the United States will not get away with massive deficit spending indefinitely without paying serious consequences. We the People want to see Congress spend more responsibly, so we should clamor for a balanced budget amendment. With the full implementation of *The Albert Plan*, we will see sustained unprecedented economic growth that will allow us to build an accumulated surplus, which will permit us to implement a balanced budget amendment, but it will take some time to get there.

Federal expenditures shall not exceed revenue unless approved by a two-thirds vote of both houses of Congress, and in all such cases, deficit spending shall be funded by the accumulated surplus.

– Proposed Constitutional Amendment Language

Line-Item Veto Amendment

Congress gave the line item veto power to the president back in the 1990s and the Supreme Court struck it down, doing a great disservice to our nation. We the People can reverse the Supreme Court decision by compelling Congress or the states to propose and ratify a constitutional amendment giving the president the line-item veto. The president would then be able to veto specific spending provisions from an omnibus spending bill without derailing the bill entirely. Limits on the length of bills should also be imposed upon Congress in order to eliminate bills that our representatives cannot even read before being required to vote on them.

Giving the president the opportunity to eliminate pork from spending bills makes too much sense to be acceptable to the establishment political class. Or perhaps they simply don't want to give up the power to buy each other off with the promise of votes in favor of ridiculous spending proposals. If Congress chooses to override a line item veto spending proposal, they should do so on the record so that voters at home could hold them accountable. We the People should also hold Congress accountable by requiring that all votes are conducted as rollcall votes and that sufficient time for public comment is given to all bills prior to a vote.

Congressional Term Limits Amendment

We the People should clamor for a term limits amendment that will limit Senators to two terms, and congressmen to four terms. Experience has shown us that we should reject the argument that we already have term limits at the ballot box every two years, for that method of limiting terms has proven ineffectual. Some make the valid argument that the administrative state with bureaucrats that are hard to terminate is where the real problem lies. We the People have a solution for that problem too!

Senators shall serve no more than two terms, and congressmen shall serve no more than four terms, including partial terms served.

– Proposed Constitutional Amendment Language

Presidential Term Limit Amendment

It would be a wonderful thing if a newly elected President could simply focus on doing the best job possible in a six-year term instead of thinking about how decisions will affect prospects for reelection. It would also be a benefit to the party in power to free other leaders of that party to lay the groundwork for potential campaigns for the office of President during the last two years of an administration instead of deferring to the current president, who may not be the best choice for the party or the country.

Election of any person to the office of President shall be limited to one term of six years. No person who has acted as President for more than two years of the term to which another person was elected President shall be elected to the office of President.

– Proposed Constitutional Amendment Language

The opposition party would benefit, as they will have a better shot at having their candidate elected President during the next election. We the People benefit, because we know that we will not be stuck with the person just elected president for more than one term. We will benefit greatly by transferring power from the federal government back to the states and substantially reducing the power of the office of the President. Doing so will benefit all Americans except for those in the entrenched establishment political class.

Impeachment Amendment

Given that the intent of the framers to structure the impeachment process in a way that would avoid partisan political impeachments has failed several times, we should permit the House of Representatives to impeach a federal official for any reason, including partisan political reasons. The best we can do is increase the threshold to two-thirds of House members, and simply require that no reason for impeachment be given.

Any federal officer may be impeached for any reason, but only upon the Concurrence of two-thirds of the Members of the House of Representatives, and any federal officer thus impeached may only be convicted and removed from office, likewise for any reason, upon the Concurrence of two-thirds of the Members of the Senate.

– Proposed Constitutional Amendment Language

With no need to prove a basis for impeachment, the path to impeachment will be expedited, and the evil intent of nefarious actors will be laid bare. Severe political repercussions will accrue to the party of the political hacks that pursue baseless impeachments. It is very unlikely that such partisan political impeachments will succeed in the house and in the Senate, and equally unlikely that such actors will gain any traction by protracted hearings and trials geared to sway public opinion.

One nuance of my proposed constitutional amendment is that it would require two thirds of the members of the house to impeach, not just two thirds of the members present. As with the

142

threshold for two-thirds of the members of the House of Representatives, this nuance will require the Concurrence of two-thirds of the number of Senators holding office, and not simply two-thirds of the Senators present when a vote to convict or acquit is held. Changing the archaic rules of the Senate that require Senators to sit through what they sat through recently will permit Senators to not participate in a sham political impeachment trial.

Federal Employment Amendment

We the People need not argue with those that say that the real problem with the federal government is the huge administrative bureaucracy that is out of control. This problem is solved with a twofold solution. Federal employees should be employees-at-will, allowing for easier termination. Federal employees should be prohibited from joining unions, and in the context of a Year of Jubilee, pensions would be eliminated.

All federal employees shall be employed at will, shall be prohibited from collective bargaining activities, and shall receive no pension or other promise of future compensation for past services rendered.

– Proposed Constitutional Amendment Language

Dramatically Reduce Federal Spending

The more significant opportunity to reduce the size of the administrative state is to dramatically reduce federal spending as proposed by *The Albert Plan*. Opportunities abound for reducing federal spending by extracting the federal government from all activities not authorized by the enumerated powers granted to the federal government by Article 1 Section 8 of the Constitution.

Congress has not unlimited powers to provide for the general welfare, but only those specifically enumerated.

– Thomas Jefferson

The powers not delegated to the United States by the Constitution, nor prohibited by it to the States, are reserved to the States respectively, or to the people.

– United States Constitution, Tenth Amendment

Most of the problems that our country faces will be resolved if We the People compel our elected officials to restore the balance of powers originally intended by the founders by respecting the 10th Amendment and simply limiting the federal government to the powers enumerated in the Constitution. We the People must clamor for cutting 75% to 90% of non-defense spending by the federal government.

If we can get the federal government out of all activities that are not expressly authorized by the Constitution, we will not only unleash the new American economy, states will have freedom to differentiate themselves by exercising authority over larger areas of governance that will give citizens of the United States the opportunity to choose between conservative governance and socialist governance.

RESTORE PROPERTY RIGHTS

One of the greatest impediments to economic growth is the aggressive implementation of restrictive zoning laws by local governments that severely limit real estate development. Property use restrictions should only be limited by life-safety issues.

It would be nice to take care of the problem by constitutional amendment or federal law, but at this time, let's assume that it is a power reserved to states, and it is up to We the People of each state to compel our states to limit property use restrictions such as zoning laws. Any state that eliminated property taxes and limited any property restrictions to life-safety issues would have a tremendous competitive advantage over states that do not.

We should all be advocates for prudent environmental stewardship, but We the People should also clamor for federal, state and local governments to bring an abrupt end to the radical environmentalist actions that have been foisted upon property owners throughout the country.

The Constitution only grants the federal government the authority to own property that is needed to build forts, magazines, arsenals, dockyards and other buildings that are needed for the operation of the federal government. We the People recognize that "other buildings" would justify more federal property than the original list, but the federal government owns approximately 20% of land in the United States, including more than half of the land in some Western states

We the People should clamor for the federal government to eliminate the Bureau of Land Management and transfer all excess federal lands to the states. Additionally, we must call for an end to the abuse of the Antiquities Act, whereby vast quantities of land have been designated monuments. All of these efforts have deprived Americans of land with which to live productive lives.

If We the People are successful in removing all of the federal and state imposed impediments and restrictions upon property, and we are successful in implementing much of *The Albert Plan*, we will see unprecedented economic growth and prosperity. As we battle the entrenched establishment political class and their globalist puppet masters for our economic liberty, We the People must be equally diligent in guarding against the federal government trying to limit our right to own and use money, or money substitutes of any type, or to enter into barter transactions.

FREE-MARKET HOUSING

The Great Reset, which will usher in the New World Order planned by the global elites, will see a dramatic reduction in the ownership of private property by the 90% of the population at the bottom of the economic pecking order. Elites are already preaching the notion that people in the future will not own anything, but will be happier. That raises the obvious question: who will own everything? No doubt, global elites will own everything.

The Biden Regime has quickly pursued the path of the managed decline of the United States, doubling down on the progress made by the Obama-Biden administration. Hedge funds and private equity firms have been gobbling up single-family homes around the country, as home prices have escalated dramatically and rents have gone up. It's pretty obvious what the global elites have in store for the vast majority of serfs if they succeed in their tyrannical plan for global domination.

If We the People, the clamoring majority, are successful in preempting The Great Reset, and are successful in implementing most of the elements of *The Albert Plan*, we will see an unleashing of free-market capitalism, and the restoration of personal and economic liberty to all Americans. This will manifest itself in a dramatic way in the unleashing of free-market housing in states that embrace and implement *The Albert Plan*.

When we decouple from China, there will be a resurgence of manufacturing jobs, and the deemphasizing of cities that is taking place will lead to job creation in "flyover" country. The movement away from cities will escalate as health insurance is either eliminated or decoupled from employment and states abandon public education in favor of free-market education. People will be more inclined to leave their jobs and start businesses, unfettered by the necessity of living close to certain schools.

States that eliminate property taxes and limit the restrictions on the use of property to life safety issues will be very attractive to those leaving cities and liberal states to establish businesses. People will be free to pursue innovative housing solutions, unfettered by restrictive policies by local governments that have choked off the supply of housing. An abundance of housing will be built, and in combination with natural deflation, owning a house will be very easy for anyone that desires to own a house, and those that don't would enjoy much more attractive rents. These changes would add rocket fuel to the unleashing of free-market housing, and millions of young people would enjoy personal and economic liberty as they pursue housing solutions limited only by their imagination.

The implementation of a year of Jubilee, the elimination of the Fed and fractional banking, the outlawing of debt, and allowing the direct investment by retail investors in block chain enabled equities that are not regulated by the SEC would be a death blow to the plans for global elites to establish a New World Order. Asset prices will plummet and gradual deflation will eliminate FOMO, the fear of missing out that compel so many people to buy homes when market prices have peaked.

The proliferation of innovative housing solutions unleashed by free-market housing will permit the construction of villages of tiny homes, or the addition of tiny homes on existing properties. These types of housing solutions will dramatically increase the supply of affordable housing where it is needed most. The dismantling of the welfare state will allow people trapped in low income housing where there are no jobs to pick up and move where they can find good jobs, which will depopulate Democrat plantations. That is why the Democrat party will vigorously oppose every element of *The Albert Plan.*

REVIVE THE MIDDLE CLASS

The net result of the full implementation of *The Albert Plan* will be an astonishing revival of the middle class in the United States. Our nation can return to a time when, fifty years ago, a middle-class family of four could live very comfortably with only one income.

Government policy and the greed of crony capitalists have choked off the opportunity for the "little guy" to pursue the American dream. The manipulation of markets has deprived the common man of enjoying the fruits of his labor and the natural deflation that should have been making life more affordable for the last half-century, instead of putting the American dream virtually out of reach for young people starting families today.

The middle class has taken a beating in recent decades, and young people have lost the hope and incentive of forming families. Government policy has become anti-family, and We the People must clamor for that to change. In addition to all of the other proposed changes, the implementation of a tax credit for the parents of all children would encourage young people to start families.

We the People must reject the Democrat approach to assisting single mothers and lower income families that is unfair and discriminatory to most young people. We the People should advocate for child tax credits to be extended to all parents of children under eighteen, regardless of need or income. Many factors have contributed to a drop in the birth rate in the United States, and this idea would reverse that trend.

Young people starting families and having children should be our preferred option for sustaining our population. The tax credit of $500 per month for each child under eighteen, regardless of household income, will cost much less than continuing immigration at an unsustainable rate, and would favor American citizens. The amount of the tax credit could be reduced once prices stabilize and gradual deflation kicks in. This isn't your typical conservative idea, but it seems to be a more appropriate "investment" than what Democrats typically want to "invest" in, and it would go a long way in reviving the middle class.

EIGHT

Next Steps

PROMOTE THE ALBERT PLAN AND ORGANIZE FREEDOM CELLS

Where there is no vision, the people perish.

— Proverbs 29:18

Our nation is in greater distress than we have seen since our founding. Some might scoff at this assertion, but it is my earnest belief that enemies, foreign and domestic, and numerous other factors, contribute to the peril that our nation is in. Could it be possible that the Americans experiment is over?

I am confident and optimistic, however, that if We the People organize in sufficient numbers and implement the elements of *The Albert Plan*, that we will not only save our Republic, we will see a renewal of American exceptionalism, and a rebirth of personal and economic liberty. We the People can do this if we each wage our own "campaign of one" to do what Albert Einstein said is our duty: for each of us to do our share to defend the Constitution.

ORGANIZE FOR ACTION

Each of us has the opportunity to conduct our own "campaign of one." I am personally "all in" in the liberty movement, and will conduct my "campaign of one" to make *The Albert Plan* "a thing," and to make Freedom Cells "a thing." I consider it my mission, indeed my calling, to educate, organize, inspire, and mobilize 30 million Minutemen to save our constitutional Republic. Part of my mission is to create content and tools that like-minded patriots like you can use to conduct your own "campaign of one."

149

As I considered how We the People should organize to save our Republic, I recognized that it is necessary to organize around a specific plan based upon a shared vision. Since no such bold, comprehensive, transformational plan existed, I articulated the plan in *The Albert Plan to Save America*. I improved upon the plan and added the 2020 Freedom Cell Survey in *The Albert Plan to Save America: 2020 Edition*. I gave my chapter on election integrity a higher priority in the 2020 edition, but the 2020 Election Farce required that I publish this book.

FreedomCells.com

If you agree with what I've written, and with what I have to say in videos that I produce, please join freedomcells.com and invite other like-minded patriots to also join. I will be publishing content on the site, and will make books and tools available, but the primary functionality that I am building into the site is for members to be able to organize and communicate with each other.

Members can join the United States Freedom Cell and the Freedom Cell for their state and congressional district. Members can also form or join Freedom Cells for their election precinct, State House District, state Senate District, and any others that members want to create. Forums will be started for members to express their views on specific topics, and members will be able to communicate with each other. I just ask for your patience as I work with early adopters to beta test the site. I hope that members will find it to be a useful tool, and lots of fun.

The most impactful Freedom Cell we can participate in is our local election precinct Freedom Cell, but those precinct Freedom Cells need to be rolled up into Freedom Cells for a county or congressional district. As we seek to hold meetings to get on the same page with the specifics of the plan and the vision behind the plan in these larger Freedom Cells, We the People can create rallies that will take what Donald Trump did with his rallies to a new level.

Faith and Freedom Fridays

We the People around the country have had Faith and Freedom rallies for years. What I have a vision for, and would like to enlist everyone involved in forming up Freedom Cells around the country to do, is to start having Freedom Cell meetings every Friday that we call "Faith and Freedom Friday." Holding Freedom Cell Faith and Freedom Friday rallies could also become "a thing." People that attend Trump rallies are not just there to see President Trump; they are there to see each other.

We the People could have Faith and Freedom Friday meetings that feature local people at each meeting as speakers instead of relying upon a limited pool of "stars" that seem to be invited to all of the meetings being held around the country. This idea occurred to me when I was talking about the liberty movement with my mechanic while leaning over the hood of my car. He went on a two or three minute rant that was inspiring to me, giving me goosebumps! Sometimes we are most inspired by ordinary people saying and doing extraordinary things.

What I have a vision for is that God-fearing, patriotic Americans will get on the same page and clamor for the same things during Faith and Freedom Friday meetings or rallies across the country. Someone traveling around would inquire as to where the Friday meetings are being held. Just like Alcoholics Anonymous has groups meeting every night of the week all over the country that people can find, and Rotary clubs have monthly meetings that are posted as you enter a town, Faith and Freedom Fridays can become "a thing." We the People can make it so!

Lockstep Lovers of Liberty

I have a vision for Faith and Freedom Friday rallies, or whatever form of future rallies that We the People choose to embrace, will sometimes be connected by simulcast technology that will have several key venues with keynote speakers that will be seen by those attending all the connected rallies simultaneously. A key element of *The Albert Plan* is that, through a tool like the 2020 Freedom Cell Survey, We the People will be in 70% agreement or more on each point of the plan.

When We the People have rallies, and 70% are cheering each particular point, the left will think that we are all in lockstep, even though only 70% may be in agreement on each particular point. When the Democrats, the leftists, the Marxists, the globalists, and all of the Lockstep Liars that want to destroy our country see thousands of patriots cheering on each point, they will start calling us Lockstep Lovers of Liberty.

PRECINCT STRATEGY

In both editions of *The Albert Plan*, I laid out how We the People can overwhelm and transform the Republican Party by forming Freedom Cells that function as the Freedom Caucus of the Republican Party all the way from the local voting precinct to the Republican National Committee. Arizona attorney Dan Schultz has been advocating for what he calls "The Precinct Strategy" in Arizona since about 2009. Steve Bannon hosted Dan on his *War Room* podcast, and together they made quite an impact on Republican Party precinct reorganizations around the country in 2021. Other people have promoted the precinct strategy, but Schultz and Bannon made it "a thing" in 2021.

Dan Schultz provides a lot of tools and useful information on his website, precinctstrategy.com. We both advocate for a peaceful takeover of the Republican Party by America-first conservatives, but there are some around the country that used the precinct strategy in a very aggressive "torches and pitchforks" kind of way. Most of the new people engaging in precinct reorganizations would have been very willing to take the approach that Schultz and I advocate for, but were led astray by people that don't fully understand what decentralized and distributed organizing looks like.

In my view, the 2021 precinct reorganization fueled by Bannon and Schultz is a warm-up for doing it the right way in 2023. If We the People use the 2020 Freedom Cell survey to vet each other, we can weed out the entrenched establishment political class types that tend to hold the positions of power in the Republican Party. I hesitate to call them "leadership" positions, because most of those in positions of power are not true leaders.

Many that agree with a large percentage of the 2020 Freedom Cell Survey will reveal that they are members of the establishment when they object to the dramatic increase in new membership and the decentralized and distributed structure of Freedom Cells. Some will even object to having separate meetings. There are many of us in the Republican Party that are anti-establishment, America-first conservatives who will embrace what We the People are trying to do to overwhelm and transform the Republican Party.

There is much that We the People can do to save our Republic if we organize 30 million Minutemen to join Freedom Cells, but the key to the strategy is for each to become a member of their voting precinct Freedom Cell. The Precinct Strategy is the key to getting organized, but it will work best if we are all on the same page behind a bold, comprehensive, transformational plan like the *Albert Plan,* or a plan of similar magnitude and direction.

Dan Schultz points out that there are about 400,000 precinct committeemen billets nationwide, but only half of them are filled. He is advocating that conservatives fill those empty positions, but if We the People mobilize an average of fifty Minutemen for every single position at precinct reorganization, we will easily overwhelm and transform the Republican Party without having to so much as raise our voices. Precinct Freedom Cells roll-up into County, State House District, State Senate District, and Congressional District Freedom Cells, which can exert tremendous influence over fielding and vetting candidates, elections, and holding candidates accountable in those election jurisdictions.

EXPOSE THE 2020 ELECTION FARCE

We the People must tirelessly work to expose the 2020 Election Farce, while simultaneously clamoring for our legislatures in each state to immediately discontinue the use of electronic voting machines or electronic tabulation machines. At a minimum, each state that hears our voice should implement voting by a single paper ballot for each decision to be made in the 2022 federal election that could be easily counted after the polls close. Each congressional district would have only one or two decisions to be made, depending upon whether or not that state has a senator up for election.

We should get behind the growing movement demanding a full forensic audit in each of the fifty states, not just the six gray states on the cover of this book. David Clements, a law professor from New Mexico, is leading one of several groups on Telegram that has chapters in every state calling for a full forensic audit in that state. We should support such efforts, because even though we will never know the whole truth, we can certainly expose much more truth about what happened in the 2020 election for all to see.

SUPPORT WARRIORS AND GLADIATORS

There are thousands of warriors and gladiators that are working around the country to expose the 2020 Election Farce and to restore election integrity, and they need our support. Each of us has time, talent, and treasure in different measure, and it is important that we use what God has given us to support "the man in the arena." Since the 2020 election, the RNC has reportedly raised over $200 million to fight for election integrity, but has done nothing to financially support the Maricopa full forensic audit.

In addition to supporting warriors and gladiators, We the People must actively resist tyrants and villains. We are in the midst of a Marxist coup. We are in a battle for truth. Liberalism is political correctness embracing a lie, and we need to forcefully expose the lie. We must expose lockstep liars for what they are. Democrats are in a fight to the death, and we need to wake up and fight back.

EDUCATE YORSELF, AND OTHERS

All education is ultimately self-education. Nothing is learned if the student does not want to learn and is not actively engaged in the learning process. The cost of education should approach near-zero as we can see from how much education is available at no cost online with the explosion of the body of knowledge and the ease with which that knowledge can be disseminated. This is how we can easily dismantle the public education system and have a better education system at dramatically lower cost.

Take advantage of what you can learn online, and from others. There are also many groups that have training modules available at no cost or low-cost that each of us can avail ourselves of to learn how to become more productive in political activism, and you don't have to agree with everything the group believes. Remember that political activism is the pursuit of a disproportionate share of influence, and embrace that as something that is necessary and good.

Reach out to Democrats and encourage them to flee the party of division, destruction, and death. The Democrat party is on a path to self-destruction, and we can help them do it by reaching out to those that are waking up to the destruction of liberty and all that is good by the Marxists that have taken over the Democrat party. Use *The Albert Plan to Save America: 2020 Edition*, the 2020 Freedom Cell Survey, and the Election Integrity Survey as tools to show disaffected Democrats how they can pull on the same end of the rope with us to save our constitutional Republic.

The best way that I can see to organize tens of millions of like-minded patriots to get on the same page in order to move as one, and speak as one, is if patriots like you will help make *The Albert Plan* "a thing" and Freedom Cells "a thing" by having "come, let us reason together" discussions.

Dedicate yourself to being a truth seeker a truth speaker. Show some intellectual curiosity and pierce the cover of darkness that nefarious characters would impose upon all of us. According to Ecclesiastes 3:3, there is "a time to break down, and a time to build up." We the People clearly need to do some breaking down of the big government that has encroached upon our liberties. It has been said that when the people fear the government, there is tyranny, but when the government fears the people, there is liberty. In order to save our Republic, We the People must restore a proper fear of the people in the hearts of those in government. If we don't take our country back, who will? If not now, when?

Is there not a cause?

Election Integrity Survey

Fellow concerned patriot: please place a checkmark to the left of the number of each question that you agree with, and a large X or "No" to the left of the number of each question that you disagree with. If you are in agreement that We the People must clamor for the Congress and state legislatures to take immediate action to restore election integrity, please share this survey with others and ask them to read *The Albert Plan to Restore Election Integrity*.

1. Do you agree that Democrats have a long history of committing election fraud, and that Republicans have allowed them to get away with it and to also expand election fraud opportunities for too long?

2. Do you agree that Democrats and other nefarious actors coordinated their efforts on an unprecedented scale during the 2020 election cycle, and that the 2020 election results were completely fraudulent?

3. Do you agree that Democrats are attempting to institutionalize election fraud through legislation proposed by HR-1?

4. Do you agree that We the People should demand that state and federal legislatures immediately take every conceivable step to restore election integrity?

5. Do you agree that Democrats use an "all of the above" strategy to undermine election integrity and commit election fraud, and that We the People should respond with an "all of the above" strategy to restore election integrity?

6. Do you agree that we should decouple federal elections from state & local elections by prohibiting other elections from being held within sixty days of Federal Election Day?

7. Do you agree that we should use fingerprints or other biometric means to confirm the legal status of all persons in the United States?

8. Do you agree that we should require voter registration by congressional district and voting precinct thirty days prior to a federal election?

9. Do you agree that we should require the publication of a list of all eligible voters by congressional district and voting precinct thirty days prior to a federal election?

10. Do you agree that we should require in-person voting on Federal Election Day, with no early voting, and with only very limited absentee voting?

11. Do you agree that absentee voters should cast their ballots in person at authorized polling locations that forward absentee ballots by secure courier to appropriate congressional districts?

12. Do you agree that voter identity and eligibility should be confirmed at the polling location by photo ID and fingerprint or other biometric means if the voter has no fingers?

13. Do you agree that voters should cast one paper ballot for each race in a federal election, white for a congressional race, pink for a Senate race, and light blue for a presidential race?

14. Do you agree that voters should affix their thumbprint or fingerprint to the back of each ballot prior to entering the voting booth?

15. Do you agree that the population for each election precinct should be limited to 5000 residents?

16. Do you agree that ballots should be sorted, counted and reported at each election precinct on election night after polls close?

17. Do you agree that elections at each precinct should be conducted with full transparency, with live stream video and the opportunity for the public to observe the voting and counting process from the perimeter of the voting area?

18. Do you agree that we should require the publication of a list of all actual voters by congressional district and voting precinct within three days of a federal election?

19. Do you agree that we should require the storage of ballots by precinct for one year in a storage facility for each con-

gressional district, and that ballots are destroyed after one year?

20. Do you agree that there should be severe criminal penalty for any intentional matching of the identity of the voter fingerprint on the back of the ballot with the vote cast on the front of the ballot?

21. Do you agree that state legislatures should be required to meet in session to certify the accuracy and integrity of federal election results?

22. Do you agree that We the People should reject any candidate for office that will not recognize that the 2020 election was fraudulent, and that the Biden Regime is illegitimate?

23. Do you agree that the United States has become a banana republic, and that we are no longer governed by the consent of the governed?

24. Do you agree that the best way to restore election integrity is to immediately implement this plan?

25. Do you agree that the 2020 federal election was a farce, and that immediately conducting a new federal election using this plan to restore election integrity is the best way to restore faith in our federal government?

2020 Freedom Cell Survey

Fellow concerned patriot: please place a checkmark to the left of the number of each question that you agree with, and a large X or "No" to the left of the number of each question that you disagree with. Use a pencil and save your responses, as you may change your position on some questions after having "come, let us reason together" discussions with other members of Freedom Cells that you form or join. If you can say "I can go along with that," go ahead and give the question a checkmark. Count the checkmarks, so you know what percentage you agree with. Use this survey to guide the discussions you have with likeminded patriots. Get to know the plan and your reasons for supporting each point!

A NATION IN DISTRESS

1. Do you believe that our nation is in distress?
2. Do you agree that liberalism is destroying America and that We the People should repudiate liberalism?
3. Do you agree that radical environmentalism is destroying America and that We the People should repudiate radical environmentalism?
4. Do you agree that globalism is destroying America and that We the People should repudiate globalism?
5. Do you agree that the entrenched establishment political class is destroying America and that We the People should repudiate the entrenched establishment political class?
6. Do you agree that our nation faces a clear and present danger from some within our government who are members of what is commonly referred to as "the deep state" and that We the People must be diligent in discovering the actions and intents of such nefarious actors and must vigilantly defend our constitutional Republic from those actors?
7. Do you agree that our nation faces a clear and present danger from lawless liberals in cities like Baltimore, Ferguson,

Berkeley, Charlottesville, Portland (OR), Minneapolis, and Seattle who permit lawlessness in order to further their agenda; from sanctuary cities and sanctuary states that flagrantly violate U.S. immigration law; and from elites that use their resources to foment violence?

8. Do you agree that our nation faces a clear and present danger from big technology companies and a complicit federal government that have eroded our right to privacy and threaten free speech as well as freedom of association, and that We the People should clamor for the federal government to use useful regulation to severely limit the opportunity for big tech companies to infringe upon our rights to privacy and free speech?

A CALL TO ACTION

9. Given that liberals do not have a monopoly on community organization, do you agree that We the People must rally behind a bold, comprehensive, transformational plan of action so that what has been known as the "silent majority" will become the "clamoring majority," as We the People organize ourselves to speak as one, and to move as one?

10. Do you agree that We the People should elect more representatives at all levels of government who share the values, principles and policy positions evidenced by the statements and actions of the Freedom Caucus in the U.S. House of Representatives, and who have the backbone to stand firm on principled positions, even when those positions are unpopular and even opposed by a president of the same party?

11. Do you agree that rather than form a third party in order to repudiate the entrenched establishment political class as some advocate for, We the People should form a third party within the Republican Party that functions like the House Freedom Caucus so that we may transform the Republican Party by electing transformational conservatives to all levels of party leadership, from precinct officers to county, state, and national officers?

12. Do you agree that the best way for the Republican Party to select candidates for office is through closed caucus or closed convention?

13. Do you agree that the lack of election integrity presents a clear and present danger to our constitutional Republic?

14. By constitutional amendment or otherwise, do you agree that We the People must restore election integrity by requiring confirmation by photographic and biometric identification, that each voter is a lawfully registered citizen entitled to vote, that early and absentee voting be eliminated, that paper ballots be used on Election Day with streaming video of the polling locations and other available means used to assure election transparency and integrity?

RESTORE FEDERALISM

15. Do you agree that the federal government has usurped the power of the states, and that We the People must restore power to the states, and to the people?

16. Do you agree that We the People should compel our states to petition Congress to call for a Convention of States to Propose Amendments?

17. Do you agree that, when a Convention of States to Propose Amendments is convened, there should be no limitation on the scope of amendments to be proposed at the convention, as any limitation on the scope of the proposal of amendments at the Convention of States to Propose Amendments would violate Article V of the Constitution?

18. Do you agree that if a proposed constitutional amendment that has been presented to the states for ratification has a deadline for ratification, that that deadline for ratification should not be extended?

19. Do you agree that, prior to the ratification of a proposed constitutional amendment by three fourths of the states, any state may withdraw its ratification of the proposed amendment, and any state that has previously voted to reject the proposed constitutional amendment may reverse its vote and ratify the proposed amendment it had rejected?

20. Since the founders intended that states may propose constitutional amendments as easily as Congress, do you agree that, by constitutional amendment, states should be permitted to directly propose amendments to the Constitution if two thirds of the state legislatures petition Congress for the proposal of an amendment with identical language, provided that ratification of such amendment by three fourths of the states be by state conventions?

21. Do you agree that the Seventeenth Amendment should be repealed?

22. By constitutional amendment or otherwise, do you agree that states should be able to nullify federal actions by the vote of two thirds of the states?

23. By constitutional amendment or otherwise, do you agree that states should have the power to remove federal officers by a two-thirds vote of the states?

24. By constitutional amendment or otherwise, do you agree that states have a natural right to secede from the union, and that that natural right to secede should be affirmed, and the manner by which states may peacefully secede should be prescribed?

RESTORE NATIONAL SOVEREIGNTY

25. Do you agree that national security should be restored as the first priority of the federal government, and that the United States should again pursue a policy of "speaking softly and carrying a big stick" by rebuilding our military and our capacity to wage war to a point that it is unmatched by any combination of our adversaries?

26. Since radical Islam has declared war on all of Western civilization, do you agree that the United States should declare war on radical Islamic terrorism and give the president, as commander-in-chief, the broad authority to conduct asymmetric military operations to fight terrorism when he deems it necessary?

27. Article IV, Section 4, of the Constitution states that the federal government shall protect the states from invasion. Do you agree that the federal government has failed in its duty

to protect the states from invasion of illegal persons and drugs along our southern border?

28. Do you agree that the United States should immediately militarize the border with Mexico by deploying active military, National Guard and citizen militia groups as needed in order to immediately secure our southern border from infiltration of illegal persons, drugs or other threats of invasion while engaging private firms to assist in the design and construction of adequate walls and technology barriers that will continue to be guarded by our military?

29. Given that the drug cartels in Mexico have infiltrated the Mexican government, have associations with ISIS and other terrorist groups and have caused great harm to our nation through the importation of drugs, do you agree that the United States should take unilateral action against the drug cartels by any means necessary?

30. Do you agree that no amnesty should be granted to illegal immigrants, and that immigration laws should be enforced in order to remove incentives for people to be here illegally and to incentivize those here illegally to self-deport?

31. Do you agree that anyone who has been granted amnesty should be denied citizenship, and hence the right to vote?

32. Do you agree that any naturalized citizen who does not assimilate or who is a proponent of sharia law, which is not compatible with our Constitution, should lose their United States citizenship and be subject to deportation?

33. In order to secure relief from the deleterious effects of the 1965 Immigration Act on the American economy and the American worker, do you agree that the United States should immediately impose a temporary moratorium on all immigration?

34. Do you agree that the United States should withdraw from the United Nations, expel the U.N. from American soil, and encourage other freedom-loving nations to also withdraw from the United Nations?

35. Do you agree that the United States has a special obligation to promote liberty and resist tyranny throughout the world?

36. Do you agree that the United States can classify nations on a freedom scale as friends, allies, adversaries, and enemies, and that we should show favor to friends and allies, and also to adversaries moving up the freedom scale toward greater liberty, and that the United States should show disfavor to those adversaries and enemies moving down the freedom scale toward greater tyranny?

37. Do you agree that the United States should set the example of moving up the freedom scale by empowering United States citizens with greater personal and economic liberty, and that we should therefore show some humility in encouraging and coaxing other nations to move up the freedom scale?

38. Do you agree that free trade and fair trade are impossible and imprudent, and that the United States should instead pursue secure, strategic trade?

39. Instead of providing so much foreign aid to and selling high-tech armaments to nations that may possibly turn against the United States in the future, do you favor the establishment of American Enterprise Zones with willing host nations that are of strategic interest to the United States whereby ninety-nine year leases are established in territories of significant size within the host country that would permit the United States military and private security forces to establish security and allow American enterprises to develop infrastructure, mining, agriculture, manufacturing, and other enterprises to the mutual benefit of the United States and the host nation?

40. Since Israel is the only democratic nation in the Middle East and our strongest ally in the region, do you agree that the United States should be unwavering in supporting Israel and the right that Israel has to national sovereignty, security, and self-determination?

41. Do you agree that President Vladimir Putin of Russia has effectively established himself as the new czar of Russia, and that despite the popularity of Putin at home, the United States should decisively check the expansionist ambitions of Russia in countries like Syria, Ukraine, and Crimea, and staunchly defend against Russian expansion in countries like

the Baltic states or any nation in Western Europe or the Western Hemisphere?

42. Do you agree that China has been waging economic warfare against the United States for decades, and that the United States must retaliate in a decisive way by pursuing secure, strategic trade and removing the constraints that the federal government has placed on us as Americans that restrict the output that We the People could produce if personal and economic liberty was restored to American citizens?

RESTORE INDIVIDUAL LIBERTY

43. By constitutional amendment or otherwise, do you agree that We the People should protect all life from conception until natural death, rendering abortion, assisted suicide and euthanasia illegal?

44. Do you believe that marriage was defined by God as between a man and a woman, was ordained by God before any government was established, is a natural right that should require no license or government approval, and should only be limited by a lawful restriction on closeness of relation?

45. Do you agree that we should propose and ratify a constitutional amendment that defines marriage as between a man and woman?

46. By constitutional amendment or otherwise, do you agree that the right of individuals and business entities to refrain from engaging in business in a manner that violates their beliefs should be protected as free speech, religious liberty and freedom of association?

47. Do you agree that the second amendment does not grant citizens the right to keep and bear arms, but rather acknowledges the natural right that individuals have to keep and bear arms?

48. By constitutional amendment or otherwise, do you agree with protecting the individual right of citizens to bear arms openly or concealed anywhere, with the exception of venues defined by Congress that have been properly secured and

have adequate armed law enforcement personnel within the venue, effectively eliminating gun-free zones?

49. Do you agree with constitutional carry and national reciprocity?

50. By constitutional amendment or otherwise, do you agree that the right to keep and bear arms should not be infringed by any tax, license, quantity limitation or registration?

51. By constitutional amendment or otherwise, do you agree that all taxes on personal, financial and real property should be eliminated, which would abolish property taxes and estate taxes?

52. By constitutional amendment or otherwise, do you agree that there should be no federal or state wage or price controls, which would eliminate the minimum wage and permit the free market to set wages and prices?

53. By constitutional amendment or otherwise, do you agree that the right to work without compulsory union membership or dues should be assured to all citizens of all states?

RESTORE LIMITED GOVERNMENT

54. By constitutional amendment or otherwise, do you agree that all income should be taxed at the same flat rate, not to exceed 15%, and that all exemptions, deductions and preferences should be eliminated?

55. By constitutional amendment or otherwise, do you agree that, in combination with a flat federal income tax not to exceed 15%, an upper limit of 5% should be established for any future national sales tax?

56. Do you agree that, in the context of a flat tax on all income not to exceed 15%, dividends paid by corporations from income that has already been taxed should not be taxable to shareholders?

57. Do you agree that we should propose and ratify a balanced budget amendment to the Constitution?

58. Do you agree that we should propose and ratify a constitutional amendment giving the president a line-item veto over expenditures proposed by Congress?

59. Do you agree that we should propose and ratify a constitutional amendment that limits the time that congressmen can serve to no more than eight years, and the time that senators can serve to no more than twelve years?

60. Do you agree that we should propose and ratify a constitutional amendment that limits the time that a president may serve to one term of six years, plus no more than two years of the term of another person that previously served as president?

61. By constitutional amendment or otherwise, do you agree that federal employees should be employees-at-will, and that they should be prohibited from forming unions for collective-bargaining purposes?

62. By constitutional amendment or otherwise, do you agree that we should abolish the IRS?

63. Do you agree that we should dramatically reduce federal spending by getting the federal government out of activities for which there is no constitutional authority, that are in fact infringements upon states' rights?

64. Do you agree that the federal government should use zero-based budgeting to reauthorize every dollar of federal spending every two years in order to reduce wasteful spending?

65. Do you agree that the primary function of the federal government is national defense and national security, and that non-defense spending should be reduced by at least 75%?

66. Do you agree that the federal government does not follow the preamble to the Constitution to promote the general welfare, but has rather unconstitutionally engaged in promoting the specific welfare of a multitude of special interests and tens of millions of individuals, leading to massive redistribution of wealth and an unhealthy dependency upon government?

67. Do you agree that the federal government has things backwards when they classify defense spending as discretionary spending, and non-defense spending as nondiscretionary?

68. Do you agree that We the People should dismantle Social Security in a manner whereby the cost and pain of doing so

will be shared by all Americans, including those that have managed to opt out of the Social Security system?

69. Do you agree that the federal government should transfer Medicare and Medicaid to the states, and that states would be prudent to dismantle Medicare and Medicaid in order to pursue free-market healthcare?

70. Do you agree that the federal government should dismantle welfare entitlement programs such as unemployment and food stamps?

71. Do you agree that the federal government should stop subsidizing cities at the expense of rural America by encouraging the development of decentralized and distributed technologies that will help all Americans instead of spending federal dollars on infrastructure projects that favor cities?

UNLEASH FREE-MARKET CAPITALISM

72. Do you agree that there is an abundance of resources on earth for free people living in free markets to produce all of the goods and services needed to enjoy life, liberty and the pursuit of happiness, and that it is tyranny, oppression and the restriction of individual liberty that create conditions leading to poverty and economic slavery?

73. Do you agree that steady, gradual deflation is the natural result of the operation of free markets, and that inflation is artificially imposed by the suppression of output and the control of capital?

74. By constitutional amendment or otherwise, do you agree that the quantity of currency that is authorized by Congress to be issued be limited based upon the quantity of gold held in reserve, and that no reduction in the quantity of gold held in reserve be permitted?

75. By constitutional amendment or otherwise, do you agree that the Federal Reserve and fractional banking should be eliminated?

76. By constitutional amendment or otherwise, do you agree that the right of American citizens to transact business with cash, gold, crypto-currencies, barter or other money substitutes should be protected?

77. Do you agree that individuals should be permitted to make direct investments in small business through block chain enabled equities in a decentralized and distributed fashion free of SEC regulation?

78. Given that global debt is spiraling out of control, with global debt increasing from approximately $146 trillion in 2007 to approximately $233 trillion in 2014, do you agree that it seems inevitable that the global financial system will collapse?

79. Given that global debt is escalating dramatically more quickly than global real wealth could possibly grow, do you agree that the massive amount of debt is effectively enslaving the vast majority of people on earth, and that it is quite likely the intended result of global elites seeking to consolidate political and economic power?

80. Do you agree that financial market discussions of negative interest rates, discussions of "bail-ins," where depositor funds are used to bail-out failed banks, and discussions of special drawing rights established by central bankers are all indicators that global elites fully expect an imminent reset of the global financial system?

81. Do you agree that We the People have the liberty to preempt the reset of the global financial system by the global elites by initiating our own reset of the global financial system that would bring the hope of economic liberty and prosperity to all instead of the tyranny and totalitarianism that would be imposed upon most people if the globalists have their way?

82. Do you agree that the United States should call for a global Year of Jubilee whereby all nations collectively agree that most nations are effectively bankrupt, and that we should all recognize that reality by resetting the global financial system by eradicating all debt and abolishing all central banks?

83. Even if other countries do not follow the lead of the United States, do you agree that the United States should declare a Year of Jubilee in the United States, whereby all debt is canceled or converted to equity, the Fed is abolished and debt is outlawed?

84. Given that the American worker and small business owners are the most important elements of any plan to revive the American economy in the context of declaring a Year of Jubilee, do you agree that in order to bring the greatest economic liberty to the largest and most important segment of the United States economy, all credit card debt, student loan debt, other unsecured consumer debt, and all mortgages and liens against all owner-occupied single-family or duplex dwelling units should be completely forgiven?

85. In the context of a Year of Jubilee, do you agree that mortgages on multifamily real estate units should be converted to an equitable sharing of equity by granting debtholders equity in each property equal to 50% of the loan-to-value ratio prior to the implementation of the Year of Jubilee, and that for the first year, landlords be prohibited from evicting any tenants that are paying rent at a percentage of household income established by Congress?

86. Given that parties in possession are the most trustworthy and competent to entrust with the challenge of keeping the wheels of the economy turning in the context of a Year of Jubilee, do you agree that, unless businesses and non-residential property owners and their creditors can voluntarily agree to converting debt to equity, debtholders should receive equity in each property or business equal to half of the percentage of debt in the original capital structure prior to the implementation of the Year of Jubilee?

87. Do you agree that, in the context of a Year of Jubilee, it would be important to eliminate wage and price rigidity and to also eliminate all future claims such as pensions, Medicaid, Medicare and Social Security so that the free market can quickly establish new wages and prices?

88. Since Congress was given the constitutional authority to establish federal courts that are inferior to the Supreme Court and to establish the jurisdiction of those courts, do you agree that Congress should use its power to reshape the federal judiciary to eliminate judicial tyranny in matters of citizenship, immigration, elections, marriage, and abortion by eliminating the jurisdiction of lower federal courts over those matters?

89. Do you agree that the United States should pursue free-market energy by permitting the free market to produce cheap, abundant, domestic energy by pursuing an "all of the above" energy policy that does not subsidize new technologies and does not penalize the fossil fuels that were used to build the greatest economic engine in history?

90. Given the much-publicized threat of an electromagnetic pulse attack upon our vulnerable centralized power grid, do you agree that federal government policy should encourage the decentralized and distributed generation of electric power, as well as the hardening of the existing power grid?

91. Do you agree that the federal government should stop defining carbon dioxide as a pollutant?

92. Do you agree that the federal government should stop imposing fuel efficiency standards for vehicles?

93. Do you agree that health insurance coverage does not mean that people will receive adequate healthcare and that Obamacare was unconstitutionally foisted upon Americans and should be repealed, permitting the free market to operate without Obamacare?

94. Do you agree that, in order to pursue free-market healthcare, government at all levels must be eliminated as third-party payers in the healthcare market?

95. Do you agree that, in order to pursue free-market healthcare, health insurance companies should be eliminated as third-party payers through federal legislation that makes health insurance policies illegal?

96. Do you agree that by eliminating government and insurance companies as third-party payers, healthcare costs will fall precipitously, that Americans will more easily afford routine healthcare, and will have a multitude of options for sharing catastrophic healthcare costs?

97. Do you agree that government at all levels should extricate themselves from education and permit We the People to pursue twenty-first century free-market education where parents are permitted to fulfill their responsibility to educate and indoctrinate their children in accordance with their values and beliefs?

98. Since learning the value of hard work is important to a well-rounded education, do you agree that children should be permitted to work, regardless of age, so long as the safety of each child is assured?

99. Do you agree that we should reverse the degradation of the right of American citizens to acquire, enjoy and dispose of property by eliminating taxes on property, limiting zoning and code enforcement laws to life-safety issues, limiting the extortion of property development, reining in the tyranny of homeowner associations, compensating property owners in imminent domain takings at twice the market value of the property taken, prohibiting civil asset forfeiture without due process, repealing tyrannical environmental laws, restoring the right of citizens to grow food and raise livestock and removing government impediments to the use of property?

100. Do you agree that the Bureau of Land Management should be abolished, and federal land that the federal government cannot constitutionally justify owning should be returned to the states?